Songs of our land, ye are with us forever;
  The power and the splendor of thrones pass away,
But yours is the might of some far flowing river,
  Through summer's bright roses, or autumn's decay.
Ye treasure each voice of the swift passing ages,
  And truth, which time writeth on leaves or on sand;
Ye bring us the bright thoughts of poets and sages,
  And keep them among us, old songs of our land.

The bards may go down to the place of their slumbers,
  The lyre of the charmer be hushed in the grave,
But far in the future the power of their numbers
  Shall kindle the hearts of our faithful and brave.
It will waken an echo in souls deep and lonely,
  Like voices of reeds by the summer breeze fanned;
It will call up a spirit of freedom, when only
  Her breathings are heard in the songs of our land.

Songs of our land! ye have followed the stranger
  With power over ocean and desert afar,
Ye have gone with our wand'rers thro' distance and danger,
  And gladdened their path like a home-guiding star.

FRANCES BROWN

What should we know,
  For better or worse,
Of the Long Ago,
  Were it not for Verse.

OLIVER ST. JOHN GOGARTY

Man is no mushroom growth of yesterday.
His roots strike deep into the hallow'd mould
Of the dead centuries; ordinances old
Govern us, whether gladly we obey
Or vainly struggle to resist their sway:
Our thoughts by ancient thinkers are controll'd,
And many a word in which our thoughts are told
Was coined long since in regions far away.

JOHN KELLS INGRAM

PROUD ARE WE IRISH

PROUD ARE WE IRISH

IRISH CULTURE AND HISTORY
AS DRAMATIZED IN VERSE AND SONG

Edited with Commentary by
JAMES MANSFIELD CLEARY

CHICAGO   QUADRANGLE BOOKS   1966

Grateful acknowledgment is made to the following for permission to reprint selections from copyrighted works:
Padraic Colum, for "A Poor Scholar of the 'Forties" and "An Old Woman of the Roads"
Coward-McCann, Inc., for "Thomas MacDonagh" by Francis Ledwidge
The Devin-Adair Company, for "To Maids Not to Walk in the Wind" by Oliver St. John Gogarty, © 1954 by Oliver St. John Gogarty
Doubleday & Company, Inc., for "Easter Week" by Joyce Kilmer, © 1917 by George H. Doran Company
A. M. Heath & Company Ltd., for "Salutation" by George William Russell
The Macmillan Company, for "The County Mayo" and "Righteous Anger" by James Stephens, © 1918 by The Macmillan Company, renewal 1946 by James Stephens; "Easter, 1916," "The Rose Tree," and "Sixteen Dead Men" by William Butler Yeats, © 1924 by The Macmillan Company, renewal 1952 by Bertha Georgie Yeats

ACKNOWLEDGMENTS

I am appreciative of the courtesy and cooperation of the Rev. Redmond Burke, Director of Libraries of De Paul University; of Ardis Kennedy, Vice President of *The Chicago Tribune*, now retired; of Padraic Colum; and of Howard H. Hays, publisher of the *Press* and *Enterprise* of Riverside, California.

PREFACE

Many years ago, before Ireland had won independence, a friend said to me: "The most exasperating thing about you *** **** Irish is your pride in being Irish. My ancestors were Germans. Think of the contributions Germans have made in literature, industry, science, music. But I don't brag of being of German descent—never think of it. My wife's folks were English. Men from that little island conquered half the world—including Ireland. Her English ancestry doesn't mean a thing to her. No other group blows off steam like you Micks. All over the world on St. Patrick's Day mobs that never saw Ireland are parading and blocking traffic. Everyone—Poles, Negroes, Chinese, Italians—everyone is expected to wear green. You all strut around bursting with pride. Pride in what? England is still ruling Ireland. What are you so proud of?"

Part of my reply was this quotation from the poem "Our Heritage," by Edward J. McPhelim:

> Dear land of sorrows, not because
> Of all thy old renown,
> But for thy lost despised cause,
> And glories trodden down,—
> See, for thy shame we cling to thee,
> Lone island of the western sea.

This book is a more complete explanation of the loyalty to Ireland of generations who have never seen "that sea-girdled, stream-silvered, lake-jeweled isle," as Oliver Wendell Holmes called it. There are millions like myself whose affectionate devotion has been inspired and maintained only by verse and song.

I was born in a small town on the border between Kansas and Nebraska. I have spent my life in Illinois, Indiana, Ohio, and Michigan. What do I know of Ireland? Mainly what the poets of Ireland have told me. Songs and verses I heard on the Nebraska prairie did something to me that no study of history, no logic, no economics, no oratory could have done.

And here they are—the simple moving sentiments in rhyme and rhythm that make Ireland and its men and women of past centuries a beloved reality to "the sea-divided Gael."

The selections that follow are not the lyrics of American and English light opera, nor are they the "stage Irish" songs of comedy and vaudeville. They are not the free verse of moderns, which is seldom remembered or quoted. And there are only a few scholarly translations from the ancient Gaelic. On the other hand, a chapter is included on a subject not adequately treated in some voluminous anthologies. It tells the story of the poets of Easter Week, 1916, whose words and whose deaths in a brief, futile failure laid the foundations for the Irish Republic of today.

Some of these poems are sweet and some are sour. Some are doggerel. Many are mere verse, not poetry. Others are worthy to be included in any anthology of the great poetry of all time. All are memorable, quotable Irish Irish. Here are the words that led men to die for Ireland. Here are the words of men who died for Ireland.

JAMES MANSFIELD CLEARY

CONTENTS

Note: Portions of poems given in the commentary are not listed here.

HUMOR   114

INVECTIVE   123

PROUD ARE WE IRISH

THE GAELS

Robert M. Hutchins, when President of the University of Chicago, gave St. Patrick and his successors credit for saving Western civilization from complete annihilation by the barbarian invasions which swept over continental Europe. He said:

> If with St. Patrick Christian civilization had not found a refuge in Ireland, no man can say where it would be today. There it flourished as nowhere else in the medieval world. In our whole civilization and in our religion, the debt we owe these men beginning with St. Patrick cannot be overestimated. In particular do we owe Ireland the literature of the English-speaking world.

> When the Church of Britain fell into decay because of the Pagan Saxon invasion, Irish missionaries restored the Church and Christianity. The earliest Christianity of Scotland came entirely from Ireland. It was the Irish who taught the Saxon how to write, and it is in the Irish hand that all the first Anglo-Saxon manuscripts are written. To the Irish all of the Anglo-Saxon world is indebted for the birth of English literature.

The following tribute to St. Patrick was written by the voice of New England, John G. Whittier:

ST. PATRICK

Saint Patrick, slave to Milcho of the herds
Of Ballymena, wakened with these words:
"Arise and flee
Out of the house of bondage and be free."

Glad as a soul in pain who hears from heaven
The angels singing of his sins forgiven,
And, wondering, sees
His prison opening to their golden keys.

He rose a man, who laid him down a slave,
Shook from his locks the ashes of the grave,
And outward trod
Into the glorious liberty of God.

He cast the symbols of his shame away,
And, passing where the sleeping Milcho lay,
Though back and limb
Smarted with wrong, he prayed, "God pardon him."

So he went forth; but in God's time he came
To light on Uilline's hills a holy flame;
And, dying, gave
The land a Saint that lost him as a slave.

O dark, sad millions, patiently and dumb
Waiting for God, your hour, at last, has come,
And freedom's song
Breaks the long silence of your nights of wrong!

Arise and flee! Shake off the vile restraint
Of ages; but like Ballymena's Saint,
The oppressor spare!
Heap only on his head the coals of prayer.

4

Go forth, like him! Like him return again
To bless the land whereon in bitter pain
Ye toiled at first,
And heal with freedom what your slavery cursed!

KUNO MEYER

Translated from the Gaelic

ST. PATRICK'S BREASTPLATE

Kuno Meyer (1859-1919) was born and died in Germany but spent much of his life in Ireland. He was a student of Gaelic and made inspired translations into English. "St. Patrick's Breastplate" is also known as "The Deer's Cry" because of the tradition that the breastplate caused assassins lying in wait for Patrick and his followers to see them as a herd of deer and let them pass.

I arise to-day
Through the strength of heaven:
Light of sun,
Radiance of moon,
Splendor of fire,
Speed of lightning,
Swiftness of wind,
Depth of sea,
Stability of earth,
Firmness of rock.

I arise to-day
Through God's strength to pilot me:
God's might to uphold me,
God's wisdom to guide me,
God's eye to look before me,
God's ear to hear me,
God's word to speak for me,
God's hand to guard me,

God's way to lie before me,
God's shield to protect me,
God's host to save me
From snares of devils,
From temptations of vices,
From every one who shall wish me ill,
Afar and anear,
Alone and in a multitude.

Christ to shield me to-day
Against poison, against burning,
Against drowning, against wounding,
So that there may come to me abundance of reward.
Christ with me, Christ before me, Christ behind me,
Christ in me, Christ beneath me, Christ above me,
Christ on my right, Christ on my left,
Christ when I lie down, Christ when I sit down, Christ
          when I arise,
Christ in the heart of every man who thinks of me,
Christ in the mouth of every one who speaks of me,
Christ in every eye that sees me,
Christ in every ear that hears me.

I arise to-day
Through a mighty strength, the invocation of the
          Trinity,
Through belief in the threeness,
Through confession of the oneness
Of the Creator of Creation.

*With Irish independence came a great burst of interest in
the history of primitive Ireland and its literature. Gaelic is
now taught in all Irish schools. Ancient poetry is given a great
deal of space in recent anthologies. A few of the most moving
verses follow.*

ENOCH O'GILLIAN

Translated from the Gaelic by T. W. H. Rolleston (1857-1920)

CLONMACNOISE

A little church was built by St. Kieran at Clonmacnoise in 548. A monastery developed which attracted students from England and the Continent. It survived ravaging and burning by Vikings and Normans but was destroyed by Henry VIII. Present monuments are two round towers, three large crosses, eight churches, and a castle.

In a quiet water'd land, a land of roses,
   Stands St. Kieran's city fair;
And the warriors of Erin in their famous generations
   Slumber there.

There beneath the dewy hillside sleep the noblest
   Of the clan of Conn,
Each below his stone with name in branching Ogham
   And the sacred knot thereon.

There they laid to rest the seven Kings of Tara,
   There the sons of Cairbre sleep—
Battle-banners of the Gael that in Kieran's plain
     of crosses
   Now their final hosting keep.

And in Clonmacnoise they laid the men of Teffia,
   And right many a lord of Breagh;
Deep the sod above Clan Creide and Clan Conaill,
   Kind in hall and fierce in fray.

Many and many a son of Conn the Hundred-fighter
   In the red earth lies at rest;
Many a blue eye of Clan Colman the turf covers,
   Many a swan-white breast.

DOUGLAS HYDE (1860-1949)

Translated from the Gaelic by the former President of Ireland

A PRAYER

Who have come have gone,
Who shall come must go,
But the Grace of God
Shall forever flow.

Gilbert Chesterton wrote:

For the great Gaels of Ireland
Are the men that God made mad,
For all their wars are merry,
And all their songs are sad.

STEPHEN GWYNN

A LAY OF OSSIAN AND PATRICK

Stephen Gwynn (1865-1950) was a member of the British Parliament for several years. He published translations from the Gaelic and wrote a history of Ireland. He was a grandson of William Smith O'Brien, leader of the 1848 rebellion. Gwynn relates how Ossian escaped when his fellow warriors of the Fianna were killed and condemned to hell. He tells how he was converted to Christianity by Patrick, and how Patrick showed him what he had escaped by his conversion. He saw all his old companions engaged in an everlasting battle seeking to fight their way from hell through an army of devils. Gull MacMorna always leads the battle sweeping away the devils with his mighty flail. Just as the battle is almost won the flail tug breaks and the Fianna retreat until Gull can replace the tug with sinews torn from the dead. Finally, Patrick says:

"Courage, O new-made Christian:
  Great is my joy in you:
I would like it ill on a day of grace
  My son should have aught to rue.

"Therefore for these your comrades
  I give you a wish today
That shall lift them out of their torment
  Into some better way.

"Speak! be bold in your asking,
  Christ is strong to redeem."
—Ossian turned to him sudden,
  Like one awaked from a dream.

His eye was fierce as an eagle's,
  And his voice had a trumpet's ring,
As when at the Fenian banquets
  He lifted his harp to sing.

"I ask no help of the Father,
  I ask no help of the Son,
Nor of the Holy Spirit,
  Ever Three in One.

"This for my only asking,
  And then let might prevail,—
Patrick, give Gull MacMorna
  An iron tug to his flail."

KING ALFRED

Translated from the Gaelic by James Clarence Mangan

ALDFRID'S ITINERARY

Alfred (or Aldfrid) is rated by the Encyclopedia Britannica as the greatest of all English kings. The Irish are proud of the fact that this Anglo-Saxon prince (whose mother was Irish) was sent to "the island of saints and scholars" for his education. His report of his travels (about the year 684) was preserved in Gaelic and has been translated by James Clarence Mangan (1803-1845).

I found in Innisfail the fair,
In Ireland, while in exile there,
Women of worth, both grave and gay men,
Many clerics and many laymen.

I travelled its fruitful provinces round,
And in every one of the five I found,
Alike in church and in palace hall,
Abundant apparel and food for all.

Gold and silver I found, and money,
Plenty of wheat and plenty of honey;
I found God's people rich in pity,
Found many a feast and many a city.

I also found in Armagh, the splendid,
Meekness, wisdom, and prudence blended,
Fasting, as Christ hath recommended,
And noble councillors untranscended.

. . .

I found the good lay monks and brothers
Ever beseeching help for others,
And in their keeping the holy word
Pure as it came from Jesus the Lord.

I found in Munster unfettered of any,
Kings, and queens, and poets a many—
Poets well skilled in music and measure,
Prosperous doings, mirth and pleasure.

I found in Connaught the just, redundance
Of riches, milk in lavish abundance;

10

Hospitality, vigor, fame,
In Cruachan's [1] land of heroic name.

I found in the country of Connall [2] the glorious,
Bravest heroes, ever victorious;
Fair-complexioned men and warlike,
Ireland's lights, the high, the starlike!

I found in Ulster, from hill to glen,
Hardy warriors, resolute men;
Beauty that bloomed when youth was gone,
And strength transmitted from sire to son.

.   .   .

I found in Leinster the smooth and sleek
From Dublin to Slewmargy's [3] peak;
Flourishing pastures, valor, health,
Long-living worthies, commerce, wealth.

I found, besides, from Ara to Glea,
In the broad rich country of Ossorie,
Sweet fruits, good laws for all and each,
Great chess-players, men of truthful speech.

I found in Meath's fair principality,
Virtue, vigor, and hospitality;
Candor, joyfulness, bravery, purity,
Ireland's bulwark and security.

I found strict morals in age and youth,
I found historians recording truth;
The things I sing of in verse unsmooth,
I found them all—I have written sooth.

---

[1] *Cruachan, or Croghan, was the name of the royal palace of Connaught.*
[2] *Tyrconnell, the present Donegal.*
[3] *Slewmargy: a mountain in the Queen's county, near the river Barrow.*

11

SEAN O'FAOLAIN

Translated from the Gaelic

FAND YIELDS CUCHULAINN TO EMER

Emer, he is your man now,
And well may you wear him,
When I can no longer hold him,
I must yield him.

Many a man has wanted me,
But I have kept my vows.
I have been an honest woman,
Under the roofs and boughs.

Pity the woman who loves a man,
When no love invites her.
Better for her to fly from love
If unloved, love bites her.

JAMES CLARENCE MANGAN

Translated from the Gaelic

THE FAIR HILLS OF EIRE, O!

Take a blessing from my heart to the land of my birth,
  And the fair Hills of Eire, O!
And to all that yet survive of Ebhear's tribe on earth,
  On the fair Hills of Eire, O!
In that land so delightful the wild thrush's lay
Seems to pour a lament forth for Eire's decay—
Alas! alas! why pine I a thousand miles away
  From the fair Hills of Eire, O!

The soil is rich and soft—the air is mild and bland,
  Of the fair Hills of Eire, O!

Her barest rock is greener to me than this rude land—
  O! the fair Hills of Eire, O!
Her woods are tall and straight, grove rising over grove;
Trees flourish in her glens below, and on her heights
        above;
O, in heart and in soul, I shall ever, ever love
  The fair Hills of Eire, O!

A noble tribe, moreover, are the now hapless Gael,
  On the fair Hills of Eire, O!
A tribe in Battle's hour unused to shrink or fail
  On the fair Hills of Eire, O!
For this is my lament in bitterness outpoured,
To see them slain or scattered by the Saxon sword.
Oh, woe of woes, to see a foreign spoiler horde
  On the fair Hills of Eire, O!

Broad and tall rise the *Cruachs* * in the golden
        morning's glow,
  On the fair Hills of Eire, O!
O'er her smooth grass for ever sweet cream and honey
        flow
  On the fair Hills of Eire, O!
O, I long, I am pining again to behold
The land that belongs to the brave Gael of old;
Far dearer to my heart than a gift of gems or gold
  Are the fair Hills of Eire, O!

The dew-drops lie bright 'mid the grass and yellow corn
  On the fair Hills of Eire, O!
The sweet-scented apples blush redly in the morn
  On the fair Hills of Eire, O!
The water-cress and sorrel fill the vales below;
The streamlets are hush'd, till the evening breezes blow,
While the waves of the Suir, noble river! ever flow
  Near the fair Hills of Eire, O!

---

* *Cruachs:* hills.

A fruitful clime is Eire's, through valley, meadow,
  plain,
  And the fair land of Eire, O!
The very "Bread of Life" is in the yellow grain
  On the fair Hills of Eire, O!
Far dearer unto me than the tones music yields,
Is the lowing of the kine and the calves in her fields,
And the sunlight that shone long ago on the shields
  Of the Gaels, on the fair Hills of Eire, O!

PATRICK HENRY PEARSE

Translated from the Gaelic

TARA IS GRASS

The world hath conquered, the wind hath scattered like
  dust
Alexander, Caesar, and all that shared their sway:
Tara is grass, and behold how Troy lieth low—
And even the English, perchance their hour will come!

KUNO MEYER

Translated from the Gaelic

EVERY STRANGER IS CHRIST

Oh King of stars!
Whether my house be dark or bright,
Never shall it be closed against any one,
Lest Christ close His house against me.

If there be a guest in your house
And you conceal aught from him,
'Tis not the guest that will be without it,
But Jesus, Mary's Son.

SEAN O'FAOLAIN

Translated from the Gaelic

STARRY SKY

O King of the starry sky
Lest thou from me withdraw Thy light,
Whether my house be dark or light,
My door shall close on none tonight.

The Statute of Kilkenny (1367) provided that an Englishman might be hanged, drawn, and quartered for marrying a Gael. One reaction was expressed in these verses by Thomas D'Arcy McGee (1825-1868) from "The Irish Wife":

I would not give my Irish wife for all the dames of the
        Saxon land;
I would not give my Irish wife for the Queen of France's
        hand;
For she to me is dearer than castles strong, or lands,
        or life—
An outlaw—so I'm near her, to love till death my
        Irish wife.

I knew the law forbade the banns—I knew my king
        abhorred her race—
Who never bent before their clans must bow before
        their ladies' grace.
Take all my forfeited domain, I cannot wage with
        kinsmen strife—
Take knightly gear and noble name, and I will keep
        my Irish wife.

THOMAS MOORE (1780-1852)

RICH AND RARE WERE THE GEMS SHE WORE

Rich and rare were the gems she wore,
And a bright gold ring on her wand she bore;
But, O her beauty was far beyond
Her sparkling gems or snow-white wand.

"Lady! dost thou not fear to stray,
So lone and lovely, through this bleak way?
Are Erin's sons so good or so cold
As not to be tempted by woman or gold?"

"Sir Knight! I feel not the least alarm,
No son of Erin will offer me harm;
For though they love woman and golden store,
Sir Knight! they love honor and virtue more!"

On she went, and her maiden smile
In safety lighted her round the Green Isle;
And blest forever is she who relied
Upon Erin's honor and Erin's pride.

An ancient Gaelic ballad gives in lengthy detail the story of
The Feast of O'Rourke. Many people have been fascinated by
the uniquely comprehensive claims of the first verse rather than
by what actually happened at the feast. The ballad, as trans-
lated by Dean Johnathan Swift, begins:

> *O'Rourke's noble fare*
> *Will ne'er be forgot*
> *By those who were there*
> *And by those who were not.*

16

Kuno Meyer pictured the boundless hospitality of the Gaelic chieftans in these words:

> *The feet of all the flies of the world*
> *are many,*
> *The treasures of Eilge are many,*
> *The stars of the sky are many,*
> *The waves of the sea are many,*
> *But the guests of O'Donnell are far*
> *more numerous.*

A GAELIC TOAST

> Health and long life to you,
> Land without rent to you,
> A child every year to you,
> And may you die in Ireland.

WILLIAM ALLINGHAM

THE FAIRIES (A Child's Song)

William Allingham (1824-1889), born in Ballyshannon, County Donegal, went to work as a clerk in his father's bank at the age of fourteen and later became a government official. This took him to London where he turned to literature and became editor of Frazer's Magazine. *He wrote more than a dozen books of songs and poems.*

> Up the airy mountain,
>   Down the rushy glen,
> We daren't go a-hunting
>   For fear of little men;
> Wee folk, good folk,
>   Trooping all together;
> Green jacket, red cap,
>   And white owl's feather!

Down along the rocky shore
  Some make their home—
They live on crispy pancakes
  Of yellow tide-foam;
Some in the reeds
  Of the black mountain lake,
With frogs for their watch-dogs,
  All night awake.

High on the hill-top
  The old King sits;
He is now so old and gray
  He's nigh lost his wits.
With a bridge of white mist,
  Columbkill he crosses,
On his stately journeys
  From Slieveleague to Rosses;
Or going up with music
  On cold starry nights,
To sup with the Queen
  Of the gay Northern Lights.

They stole little Bridget
  For seven years long;
When she came down again
  Her friends were all gone.
They took her lightly back,
  Between the night and morrow;
They thought that she was fast asleep,
  But she was dead with sorrow.
They have kept her ever since
  Deep within the lakes,
On a bed of flag-leaves,
  Watching till she wakes.

By the craggy hill-side,
  Through the mosses bare,
They have planted thorn-trees

For pleasure here and there.
Is any man so daring
  As dig one up in spite,
He shall find their sharpest thorns
  In his bed at night.

Up the airy mountain,
  Down the rushy glen,
We daren't go a-hunting
  For fear of little men;
Wee folk, good folk,
  Trooping all together;
Green jacket, red cap,
  And white owl's feather!

THOMAS MOORE

LET ERIN REMEMBER THE DAYS OF OLD

Let Erin remember the days of old,
  Ere her faithless sons betray'd her;
When Malachi wore the collar of gold
  Which he won from her proud invader;
When her kings, with standard of green unfurl'd,
  Led the Red Branch Knights to danger;—
Ere the emerald gem of the western world
  Was set in the crown of a stranger.

On Lough Neagh's bank as the fisherman strays,
  When the clear cold eve's declining,
He sees the round towers of other days
  In the wave beneath him shining;
Thus shall memory often in dreams sublime,
  Catch a glimpse of the days that are over;
Thus, sighing, look through the waves of time
  For the long-faded glories they cover.

19

THE LAND

The scenery and climate of Ireland are not threatening the tourist business of California, Switzerland, Hawaii, Florida, or the Riviera, but nothing that the advertisements report about these earthly heavens can equal the charm and thrill that Irish poets see and feel in their island.

THOMAS OSBORN DAVIS

MY LAND

Thomas Osborn Davis (1814-1845), in the last three years of his short life, wrote poems that have deeply moved the Irish people for more than a century. His father, a Welshman, was a surgeon in the Royal Artillery, his mother Irish. He graduated from Trinity College and became an attorney. Three years before his death he joined Charles Gavan Duffy and John Blake Dillon in founding The Nation, *an Irish rebel weekly, and began writing poetry for it. When Davis died in 1845, John Mitchell wrote that the fight for independence had "lost its very heart and soul." Almost a century later Yeats said that he hoped to be remembered with Davis, Mangan, and Ferguson.*

20

She is a rich and rare land;
Oh! she's a fresh and fair land;
She is a dear and rare land—
  This native land of mine.

No men than hers are braver—
Her women's hearts ne'er waver;
I'd freely die to save her,
  And think my lot divine.

She's not a dull nor cold land—
No! she's a warm and bold land;
Oh! she's a true and old land—
  This native land of mine.

Could beauty ever guard her,
And virtue still reward her,
No foe would cross her border
  No friend within her pine!

Oh, she's a fresh and fair land;
Oh, she's a true and rare land!
Yes, she's a rare and fair land—
  This native land of mine.

WILLIAM DRENNAN

ERIN

*William Drennan (1754-1820), born in Belfast, wrote the orig-
inal manifesto of the Society of United Irishmen. He was tried
for sedition but acquitted. In the following verses he originated
the phrase "Emerald Isle." Irish freedom was won a century after
his death.*

When Erin first rose from the dark swelling flood,
God bless'd the green island, and saw it was good;
The em'rald of Europe, it sparkled and shone,
In the ring of the world, the most precious stone.

In her sun, in her soil, in her station thrice blest,
With her back towards Britain, her face to the West,
Erin stands proudly insular, on her steep shore,
And strikes her high harp mid the ocean's deep roar.

But when its soft tones seem to mourn and to weep,
The dark chain of silence is thrown o'er the deep;
At the thought of the past the tears gush from her eyes,
And the pulse of her heart makes her white bosom rise.
O! sons of green Erin, lament o'er the time,
When religion was war, and our country a crime,
When man, in God's image, inverted his plan,
And moulded his God in the image of man.

.   .   .

Alas! for poor Erin that some are still seen,
Who would dye the grass red from their hatred to Green;
Yet, oh! when you're up and they're down, let them live,
Then yield them that mercy which they would not give.
Arm of Erin be strong! but be gentle as brave!
And uplifted to strike, be still ready to save!
Let no feeling of vengeance presume to defile
The cause of, or men of, the Emerald Isle.

The cause it is good, and the men they are true,
And the Green shall outlive both the Orange and Blue!
And the triumphs of Erin her daughters shall share,
With the full swelling chest, and the fair flowing hair.
Their bosom heaves high for the worthy and brave,
But no coward shall rest in that soft-swelling wave;
Men of Erin! awake, and make haste to the blest,
Rise—Arch of the Ocean, and Queen of the West!

Gaelic bards sometimes personalized Ireland as a woman. Translators used four names—Dark Rosaleen, Kathleen the Daughter of Houlahan, Dear Dark Head, and Shan Van Voght. The last means "poor old woman." The best-loved play by Yeats is "Cathleen ni Hoolihan." He also wrote of her in "Red Hanrahan's Song About Ireland." The two most quoted poems of James Clarence Mangan were "Dark Rosaleen" and "Kathleen-Ni-Houlahan," which follow:

JAMES CLARENCE MANGAN

DARK ROSALEEN

James Clarence Mangan was driven to drink and opium by a life of poverty and a tragic love affair. With only a few years of formal education, he published poems that purported to be translations from the Persian and the German, because "Hafiz is more acceptable to editors than Mangan." He took literal prosy translations from Gaelic and converted them into moving, memorable poems. Mangan did not read Gaelic. His poems listed as "from the Gaelic" were based on prose translations that had been made by John O'Donovan.

O my Dark Rosaleen,
  Do not sigh, do not weep!
The priests are on the ocean green,
  They march along the Deep.
There's wine . . . from the royal Pope
  Upon the ocean green;
And Spanish ale shall give you hope,
  My Dark Rosaleen!
  My own Rosaleen!
Shall glad your heart, shall give you hope,
Shall give you health, and help, and hope,
  My Dark Rosaleen.

Over hills and through dales
  Have I roamed for your sake;
All yesterday I sailed with sails
  On river and on lake.
The Erne . . . at its highest flood
  I dashed across unseen,
For there was lightning in my blood,
  My Dark Rosaleen!
  My own Rosaleen!
Oh! there was lightning in my blood,
Red lightning lightened through my blood,
  My Dark Rosaleen!

All day long in unrest
  To and fro do I move,
The very soul within my breast
  Is wasted for you, love!
The heart . . . in my bosom faints
  To think of you, my Queen,
My life of life, my saint of saints,
  My Dark Rosaleen!
  My own Rosaleen!
To hear your sweet and sad complaints,
My life, my love, my saint of saints,
  My Dark Rosaleen!

Woe and pain, pain and woe,
  Are my lot night and noon,
To see your bright face clouded so,
  Like to the mournful moon.
But yet . . . will I rear your throne
  Again in golden sheen;
'Tis you shall reign, shall reign alone,
  My Dark Rosaleen!
  My own Rosaleen!
'Tis you shall have the golden throne,
'Tis you shall reign, and reign alone,
  My Dark Rosaleen!

Over dews, over sands
  Will I fly for your weal;
Your holy delicate white hands
  Shall girdle me with steel.
At home . . . in your emerald bowers,
  From morning's dawn till e'en,
You'll pray for me, my flower of flowers,
  My Dark Rosaleen!
  My fond Rosaleen!
You'll think of me through Daylight's hours,
My virgin flower, my flower of flowers,
  My Dark Rosaleen!

I could scale the blue air,
  I could plough the high hills,
Oh, I could kneel all night in prayer,
  To heal your many ills!
And one . . . beamy smile from you
  Would float like light between
My toils and me, my own, my true,
  My Dark Rosaleen!
  My fond Rosaleen!
Would give me life and soul anew,
A second life, a soul anew,
  My Dark Rosaleen!

O! the Erne shall run red
  With redundance of blood,
The earth shall rock beneath our tread,
  And flames wrap hill and wood,
And gun-peal, and slogan cry,
  Wake many a glen serene,
Ere you shall fade, ere you shall die,
  My Dark Rosaleen!
  My own Rosaleen!
The Judgment Hour must first be nigh,
Ere you can fade, ere you can die,
  My Dark Rosaleen!

KATHLEEN-NI-HOULAHAN

Long they pine in weary woe, the nobles of our land,
Long they wander to and fro, proscribed, alas! and
     banned;
Feastless, houseless, altarless, they bear the exile's brand,
  But their hope is in the coming-to of
     Kathleen-Ni-Houlahan!

Think her not a ghastly hag, too hideous to be seen,
Call her not unseemly names, our matchless Kathleen;
Young is she, and fair she is, and would be crowned
     a queen,
  Were the Kings son at home here with
     Kathleen-Ni-Houlahan!

Sweet and mild would look her face, O none so sweet
     and mild,
Could she crush her foes by whom her beauty is reviled;
Woolen plaids would grace herself and robes of silk
     her child,
  If the King's son were living here with
     Kathleen-Ni-Houlahan!

Sore disgrace it is to see the Arbitress of Thrones
Vassal to a *Saxoneen* of cold and sapless bones!
Bitter anguish wrings our souls—with heavy sighs
     and groans
  We wait the Young Deliverer of
     Kathleen-Ni-Houlahan!

Let us pray to Him who holds Life's issues in his hands—
Him who formed the mighty globe, with all its thousand
     lands;

Girding them with seas and mountains, rivers deep,
      and strands,
  To cast a look of pity upon Kathleen-Ni-Houlahan!

He, who over sands and waves led Israel along—
He, who fed, with heavenly bread, that chosen tribe
      and throng—
He, who stood by Moses, when his foes were fierce
      and strong—
  May He show forth His might in saving
      Kathleen-Ni-Houlahan.

WILLIAM BUTLER YEATS (1865-1939)

RED HANRAHAN'S SONG ABOUT IRELAND

The old brown thorn trees break in two high over
      Cummen Strand,
Under a bitter black wind that blows from the left hand;
Our courage breaks like a tree in a black wind and dies,
But we have hidden in our hearts the flame out of the
      eyes
Of Cathleen, the daughter of Houlihan.

The wind has bundled up the clouds high over
      Knocknarea,
And thrown the thunder on the stones for all that Maeve
      can say.
Angers that are like noisy clouds have set our hearts
      abeat;
But we have all bent low and low kissed the quiet feet
Of Cathleen, the daughter of Houlihan.

The yellow pool has overflowed high up on Clooth-
      na-Bare,
For the wet winds are blowing out of the clinging air;

Like heavy flooded waters our bodies and our blood;
But purer than a candle before the Holy Rood
Is Cathleen, the daughter of Houlihan.

Sir Samuel Ferguson

DEAR DARK HEAD

*Samuel Ferguson (1810-1886), born in Belfast, founded the
Protestant Repeal Association in his youth, later became Queen's
counsel, and was knighted for his service as Keeper of Public
Records of Ireland.*

Put your head, darling, darling, darling,
    Your darling black head my heart above;
Oh, mouth of honey, with the thyme for fragrance,
    Who, with heart in breast, could deny you love?

Oh, many and many a young girl for me is pining,
    Letting her locks of gold to the cold wind free,
For me, the foremost of our gay young fellows;
    But I'd leave a hundred, pure love, for thee!

Then put your head, darling, darling, darling,
    Your darling black head my heart above;
Oh, mouth of honey, with the thyme for fragrance,
    Who, with heart in breast, could deny you love?

Winifred M. Letts

A SOFT DAY

*The Irish people, strange to say, are very proud of their
climate. Each rainy day in endless succession is greeted affection-*

ately as a "soft" day. It is said that when the Ark floated over Ireland only a few mountain peaks were still not submerged. From the top of Slieve na Mon in Tipperary, a lone survivor called out to Noah: "A fine soft day, glory be to God!"

The sentiment is well expressed in verse by Winifred Letts (1882-   ), who also wrote books for children and plays for the Abbey Theater.

A soft day, thank God!
A wind from the south
With honeyed mouth;
A scent of drenching leaves,
Briar and beech and lime,
White elder-flower and thyme
And the soaking grass smells sweet
Crushed by my two bare feet,
While the rain drips,
Drips, drips, drips from the leaves.

A soft day, thank God!
The hills wear a shroud
Of silver cloud;
The web the spider weaves
Is a glittering net;
The woodland path is wet,
And the soaking earth smells sweet
Under my two bare feet,
And the rain drips,
Drips, drips, drips from the leaves.

Moira O'Neill wrote from her home in the Canadian Rockies:

Wathers o' Moyle, I hear ye callin'
Clearer for half o' the world between,
Antrim hills an' the wet rain fallin'

29

Whiles ye are nearer than snow tops keen:
Dreams o' the night an' a night wind callin',
What is the half o' the world between?

Scotch Will Lithgow reported of his traveling in Ireland in
1619:

> *And this I dare avow, there are more rivers, lakes,*
> *brooks, strands, quagmaires, bogs, and marshes in this*
> *country than in all Christendom besides. In five months'*
> *space I quite spoiled six horses, and myself as tired as*
> *the worst of them.*

WILLIAM ALLINGHAM

FOUR DUCKS ON A POND

Four ducks on a pond,
A grass bank beyond,
A blue sky of spring,
White clouds on the wing:
What a little thing
To remember for years,
To remember with tears!

LADY GILBERT (ROSA MULHOLLAND)

SHAMROCKS

Lady Gilbert (Rosa Mulholland) (1855-1916) was the daughter
of a Belfast physician and the wife of a noted archaeologist. At
the age of fifteen she attempted to sell her drawings to Punch,
and when they were rejected she turned to writing. Her first

poem was illustrated by Millais. Charles Dickens became her
friend and published one of her novels in the same volume with
one of his own.

I wear a shamrock in my heart.
  Three in one, one in three—
  Truth and love and faith,
  Tears and pain and death;
O sweet my shamrock is to me!

Lay me in my hollow bed,
  Grow the shamrocks over me.
  Three in one, one in three,
  Faith and hope and charity,
  Peace and rest and silence be
With me where you lay my head:
O dear the shamrocks are to me!

THOMAS MOORE

OH, THE SHAMROCK

  Through Erin's Isle,
  To sport awhile,
As Love and Valor wander'd;
  With Wit, the sprite,
  Whose quiver bright
A thousand arrows squander'd;
  Where'er they pass,
  A triple grass
Shoots up, with dew-drops streaming,
  As softly green
  As emerald seen
Thro' purest crystal gleaming.
  Oh, the Shamrock, the green, immortal Shamrock!
  Chosen leaf

Of Bard and Chief,
Old Erin's native Shamrock!

Says Valor, "See,
"They spring for me,
"Those leafy gems of morning!"
Says Love, "No, no
"For me they grow,
"My fragrant path adorning."
But Wit perceives
The triple leaves,
And cries, "Oh! do not sever
"A type that blends
"Three godlike friends,
"Love, Valor, Wit, forever!"
Oh, the Shamrock, the green, immortal Shamrock!
Chosen leaf
Of Bard and Chief,
Old Erin's native Shamrock!

So firmly fond
May last the bond
They wove that morn together,
And ne'er may fall
One drop of gall
On Wit's celestial feather!
May Love, as twine
His flowers divine,
Of thorny falsehood weed 'em!
May Valor ne'er
His standard rear
Against the cause of Freedom!
Oh, the Shamrock, the green, immortal Shamrock!
Chosen leaf
Of Bard and Chief,
Old Erin's native Shamrock!

THOMAS MOORE

THE MEETING OF THE WATERS

There is not in the wide world a valley so sweet
As that vale in whose bosom the bright waters meet; *
O the last rays of feeling and life must depart,
Ere the bloom of that valley shall fade from my heart.

Yet it was not that nature had shed o'er the scene
Her purest of crystal and brightest of green;
'Twas not the soft magic of streamlet or hill,
O no,—it was something more exquisite still.

'Twas that friends, the beloved of my bosom, were near,
Who made every dear scene of enchantment more dear,
And who felt how the best charms of nature improve,
When we see them reflected from looks that we love.

Sweet vale of Avoca! how calm could I rest
In thy bosom of shade, with the friends I love best,
Where the storms that we feel in this cold world should
         cease,
And our hearts, like thy waters, be mingled in peace.

WILLIAM BUTLER YEATS

THE LAKE ISLE OF INNISFREE

I will arise and go now, and go to Innisfree,
    And a small cabin build there, of clay and wattles
         made;
Nine bean rows will I have there, a hive for the
         honeybee,
    And live alone in the bee-loud glade.

---

* The rivers Avon and Avoca form part of the beautiful scenery between
Rathdrum and Arklow in the county of Wicklow. These lines were suggested
by a visit to this romantic spot in the summer of the year 1807.

And I shall have some peace there, for peace comes
        dropping slow,
  Dropping from the veils of the morning to where the
        cricket sings;
There midnight's all a-glimmer, and noon a purple
        glow,
  And evening full of the linnet's wings.

I will arise and go now, for always night and day
  I hear lake water lapping with low sounds by the
        shore;
While I stand on the roadway, or on the pavements gray,
  I hear it in the deep heart's core.

*There are two popular poems about the County Mayo, one
about leaving it, the other about returning.*

Thomas Flavel

Translated from the Gaelic by George Fox

THE COUNTY OF MAYO

On the deck of Patrick Lynch's boat I sat in woeful
        plight,
Through my sighing all the weary day and weeping all
        the night.
Were it not that full of sorrow from my people forth I go,
By the blessed sun, 'tis royally I'd sing thy praise, Mayo.

When I dwelt at home in plenty, and my gold did much
        abound,
In the company of fair young maids the Spanish ale went
        round.
'Tis a bitter change from those gay days that now I'm

forced to go,
And must leave my bones in Santa Cruz, far from my own
  Mayo.

They are altered girls in Irrul now: 'tis proud they're
  grown and high,
With their hair-bags and their top-knots—for I pass their
  buckles by.
But it's little now I heed their airs, for God will have
  it so,
That I must depart for foreign lands, and leave my sweet
  Mayo.

'Tis my grief that Patrick Loughlin is not Earl in Irrul
  still,
And that Brian Duff no longer rules as Lord upon the
  Hill;
And that Colonel Hugh MacGrady should be lying dead
  and low,
And I sailing, sailing swiftly from the county of Mayo.

JAMES STEPHENS (1882-1950)

Translated from the Gaelic

THE COUNTY MAYO

Now with the coming in of the spring the days will
  stretch a bit,
And after the Feast of Brigid I shall hoist my flag and go,
For since the thought got into my head I can neither
  stand nor sit
Until I find myself in the middle of the County of Mayo.

In Claremorris I would stop a night and sleep with
  decent men,
And then go on to Balla just beyond and drink galore,

And next to Kiltimagh for a visit of about a month,
     and then
I would only be a couple of miles away from Ballymore.

I say and swear my heart lifts up like the lifting of a tide,
Rising up like the rising wind till fog or mist must go,
When I remember Carra and Gallen close beside,
And the Gap of the Two Bushes, and the wide plains of
     Mayo.

To Killaden then, to the place where everything grows
     that is best,
There are raspberries there and strawberries there and all
     that is good for men;
And if I were only there in the middle of my folk my
     heart could rest,
For age itself would leave me there and I'd be young
     again.

MOIRA O'NEILL

CORRYMEELA

Over here in England I'm helpin' wi' the hay,
And I wisht I was in Ireland the livelong day;
Weary on the English hay, an' sorra take the wheat!
Och! Corrymeela, an' the blue sky over it.

There's a deep dumb river flowin' by beyont the heavy
     trees,
This livin' air is moithered wi' the hummin' o' the bees;
I wisht I'd hear the Claddagh burn go runnin'
     through the heat,
Past Corrymeela, wi' the blue sky over it.

The people that's in England is richer nor the Jews,

There's not the smallest young gossoon but thravels in
      his shoes!
I'd give the pipe between me teeth to see a barefut
      child,
Och! Corrymeela, an' the low south wind.

Here's hands so full o' money an' hearts so full o' care,
By the luck o' love! I'd still go light for all I did go bare.
"God save ye, colleen dhas," I said; the girl she thought
      me wild!
Fair Corrymeela, an' the low south wind.

D'ye mind me now, the song at night is mortial hard
      to raise,
The girls are heavy goin' here, the boys are ill to plase;
When ones't I'm out this workin' hive, 'tis I'll be back
      again—
Aye, Corrymeela, in the same soft rain.

MICHAEL W. BALFE

KILLARNEY

*Michael William Balfe (1808-1870), a violinist at the age of
nine, became conductor of Her Majesty's Theater in London.*

By Killarney's lakes and fells,
   Emerald isles and winding bays,
Mountain paths, and woodland dells
   Memory ever fondly strays.
Bounteous nature loves all lands,
   Beauty wanders everywhere,
Footprints leaves on many strands,
   But her home is surely there.
     Angels fold their wings and rest
     In that Eden of the west,

Beauty's home, Killarney,
Ever fair, Killarney.

Innisfallen's ruin'd shrine
   May suggest a passing sigh,
But man's faith can ne'er decline
   Such God's wonders floating by
Castle Lough and Glena Bay,
   Mountains Tore and Eagle's nest,
Still at Muckross you must pray,
   Though the monks are now at rest.
      Angels wonder not that man
      There would fain prolong life's span,
      Beauty's home, Killarney,
      Ever fair, Killarney.

No place else can charm the eye
   With such bright and varied tints:
Every rock that you pass by
   Verdure borders or besprints.
Virgin there the green grass grows,
   Every morn Spring's natal day,
Bright hued berries daff the snows,
   Smiling winter's frown away.
      Angels often pausing there,
      Doubt if Eden were more fair,
      Beauty's home, Killarney,
      Ever fair, Killarney.

Music there for echo dwells,
   Makes each sound a harmony,
Many voic'd the chorus swells,
   Till it faints in ecstasy.
With the charmful tints below
   Seems the Heaven above to vie,
All rich colors that we know
   Tinge the cloud wreaths in that sky.
      Wings of angels so might shine,

Glancing back soft light divine,
Beauty's home, Killarney,
Ever fair, Killarney.

Francis Sylvester O'Mahony (1805-1866) was born in Cork. He was educated for the Jesuit priesthood in France and Italy but soon gave up his clerical functions and spent his life in several countries—mainly in London as a writer, editor, and friend of Thackeray, Coleridge, Southey, Carlyle, Moore, and Dickens. His articles as Rome correspondent of The Daily News *were published under the title, "Facts and Figures from Italy by Don Jeremy Savonarola, Benedictine Monk." Most of his work was signed "Father Prout."*

"Father Prout" translated Moore's Melodies into what purported to be originals in Greek, Latin, Italian, and French. He then congratulated Moore on his clever plagiarisms. He translated Millikin's "Groves of Blarney" into the above four languages and added these lines which have become far better known than the original poem:

> *There is a stone there,*
> *That whoever kisses,*
> *Oh! he never misses*
> *To grow eloquent;*
> *'Tis he may clamber*
> *To a lady's chamber,*
> *Or become a member*
> *Of parliament.*
> *A clever spouter*
> *He'll soon turn out, or*
> *An out-and-outer,*
> *To be let alone.*
> *Don't hope to hinder him,*
> *Or to bewilder him,*
> *Sure he's a pilgrim*
> *From the Blarney Stone!*

For years he gave up the "O" in his name and then returned to it. Of all his writings the most popular was "The Bells of Shandon."

FRANCIS SYLVESTER O'MAHONY

THE BELLS OF SHANDON

The "Bells," the pride of Cork city, are in the steeple of Shandon Church. Where the church now stands was once an old fort or dun. Shau-Dhun is Gaelic for old fort.

With deep affection and recollection
   I often think of those Shandon Bells,
Whose sounds so wild would in days of childhood
   Fling round my cradle their magic spells.
On this I ponder where'ere I wander,
   And thus grow fonder, sweet Cork, of thee,
With thy Bells of Shandon that sound so grand
   On the pleasant waters of the River Lee.

I've heard bells chiming full many a clime in,
   Tolling sublime in Cathedral shrine,
While at a glib rate brass tongues would vibrate,
   But all their music spoke not like thine.
For mem'ry dwelling on each proud swelling
   Of the belfry knelling its bold notes free,
Made the Bells of Shandon sound far more grand
   On the pleasant waters of the River Lee.

I've heard bells tolling "Old Adrian's Mole" in
   Their thunder rolling from the Vatican;
And cymbals glorious, that swing uproarious
   In the turrets gorgeous of Notre Dame.
But thy sounds were sweeter, than the dome of Peter

Flings o'er the Tiber so solemnly;
O the Bells of Shandon sound far more grand
On the pleasant waters of the River Lee.

Mary Anne Kelly

TIPPERARY

*Mary Anne Kelly (1836-1910) used the name "Eva" in con-
tributing poems to* The Nation. *When her rebel sweetheart, K. I.
O'Doherty, was imprisoned he was offered his freedom if he
would plead guilty. "Eva" urged him not to do so and promised
to wait for him. Eventually they were married.*

They say that your hand is fearful, that darkness is in
       your eye:
But I'll not let them dare to talk so black and bitter a lie.
O! no, *macushla storin!* bright, bright, and warm are you,
With hearts as bold as the men of old, to yourselves and
       your country true.

And when there is gloom upon you, bid them think who
       has brought it there—
Sure a frown or a word of hatred was not made for your
       face so fair;
You've a hand for the grasp of friendship—another to
       make them quake,
And they're welcome to whichsoever it pleases them most
       to take.

Shall our homes, like the huts of Connaught, be crumbled
       before our eyes?
Shall we fly, like a flock of wild geese, from all that we
       love and prize?
No! by those who were here before us, no churl shall our

tyrant be;
Our land it is theirs by plunder, but, by Brigid, ourselves
are free.

No! we do not forget the greatness did once to sweet Eriè
belong;
No treason or craven spirit was ever our race among;
And no frown or no word of hatred we give—but to pay
them back;
In evil we only follow our enemies' darksome track.

O! come for a while among us, and give us the friendly
hand;
And you'll see that old Tipperary is a loving and
gladsome land;
From Upper to Lower Ormond, bright welcomes and
smiles will spring;
On the plains of Tipperary the stranger is like a king.

Were you ever in sweet Tipperary, where the fields are
so sunny and green,
And the heath-brown Slieve-bloom and the Galtees look
down with so proud a mien?
'Tis there you would see more beauty than is on all Irish
ground—
God bless you, my sweet Tipperary, for where could your
match be found?

KATHERINE TYNAN-HINKSON

OH, GREEN AND FRESH

*Katherine Tynan-Hinkson (1861-1931) had no formal educa-
tion after leaving the Dominican convent at Drogheda at age
fourteen, but the first of her nine volumes of verse was published*

42

in 1885. She also wrote several novels and three books of literary memoirs.

Oh, green and fresh your English sod
  With daisies sprinkled over;
But greener far were the fields I trod,
  And the honeyed Irish clover.

Oh, well your skylark cleaves the blue
  To bid the sun good-morrow;
He has not the bonny song I knew
  High over an Irish furrow.

And often, often, I'm longing still,
  This gay and golden weather,
For my father's face by an Irish hill
  And he and I together.

DENIS A. MCCARTHY (? -1931)

GOING BACK

Oh, Ireland is a pleasant place when youth is in the veins,
'Tis pleasant when the sun is out, 'tis pleasant when it
      rains.
For sure the eyes of youth can pierce the thickest rain
      or mist,
And see afar the mountains by the kindly sunshine kissed.

Faith, every hill's a mountain there, and every bush a
      tree,
And every stream a river wide, and every lake a sea;
And every heart a fount of hope and faith and love and
      truth;
Oh, Ireland is the pleasant place to them that have the
      youth.

Oh, Ireland is the merry place where heads and hearts
    are young,
How many a wayside dance is there, how many a song
    is sung;
'Tis there the wildest music is and there the maddest
    mirth,
And oh, 'tis there's the softest speech was ever heard
    on earth.

Aye, sure 'tis there, I'm thinking, that the sweetest words
    are said,
And over there's the blarney that would turn the wisest
    head.
And tales of yore and fairy lore, and jesting full of joy,
Oh, Ireland is the merry place when one is but a boy.

But Ireland is a lonesome place, a strange and eerie land,
When after years of exile on its shores again you stand,
The air has lost its graciousness, the sun its golden light,
And where are all the hawthorn blooms that used to be
    so white?

And oh, the skies so gray and grim, those skies that once
    were blue,
And oh, the rain that seems to weep for friends that once
    you knew!
Ah, me, the change! Ah, me, how strange to find old
    Ireland sad,
That used to be so happy to a happy-hearted lad!

JOHN TODHUNTER

LONGING

*John Todhunter (1839-1916) was a distinguished Dublin physi-
cian as well as a poet.*

O the sunshine of old Ireland, when it lies
  On her woods and on her waters;
  And gleams through her soft skies,
Tenderly as the lovelight in her daughters'
        Gentle eyes!

O the brown streams of old Ireland, how they leap
  From her glens, and fill their hollows
  With wild songs, till charmed to sleep
By the murmuring bees in meadows, where the swallows
        Glance and sweep!

O my home there in old Ireland—the old ways
  We had, when I knew only
  Those ways of one sweet place;
Ere afar from all I loved I wandered lonely,
        Many days!

O the springtime in old Ireland! O'er the sea
  I can smell our hawthorn bushes,
  And it all comes back to me—
The sweet air, the old place, the trees, the cows, the
        thrushes
        Mad with glee.

I'm weary for old Ireland—once again
  To see her fields before me,
  In sunshine or in rain!
And the longing in my heart when it comes o'er me
        Stings like pain.

TO GOD AND IRELAND TRUE

Ellen O'Leary (1831-1889) was a sister of the famous Fenian leader, John O'Leary. She assisted in the escape from prison of James Stephens, another founder of the Fenian movement.

I sit beside my darling's grave,
    Who in the prison died,
And tho' my tears fall thick and fast,
    I think of him with pride:
Ay, softly fall my tears like dew,
For one to God and Ireland true.

"I love my God o'er all," he said,
    "And then I love my land,
And next I love my Lily sweet,
    Who pledged me her white hand:
To each—to all—I'm ever true;
To God—to Ireland—and to you."

No tender nurse his hard bed smoothed
    Or softly raised his head;
He fell asleep and woke in heaven
    Ere I knew he was dead;
Yet why should I my darling rue?
He was to God and Ireland true.

Oh! 'tis a glorious memory;
    I'm prouder than a queen
To sit beside my hero's grave,
    And think on what has been:
And, oh, my darling, I am true
To God—to Ireland—and to you.

I GIVE MY HEART TO THEE

Standish O'Grady (1846-1928) wrote a novel entitled In the Wake of King James. *This gave Hugh E. Keough, a columnist on* The Chicago Tribune, *an idea, and he changed the name of his column from "Some Off-Side Plays" to "In the Wake of the News." It has borne this name for more than fifty years under his successors, Jack Lait, Ring Lardner, Harvey Woodruff, Arch Ward, and David Condon.*

> I give my heart to thee, O mother-land—
> I, if none else, recall the sacred womb.
> I, if none else, behold the loving eyes
> Bent over on thy myriad progeny
> Who care not nor regard thee as they go,
> O tender, sorrowing, weeping, hoping land!
> I give my heart to thee, O mother-land.
>
> I give my heart to thee, O father-land,
> Fast-anchored on thine own eternal soul,
> Rising with cloudy mountains to the skies.
> O proud, strong land, unstooping, stern of rule,
> Me rule as ever; let me feel thy might;
> Let me go forth with thee now and for aye.
> I give my heart to thee, ideal land.
>
> I give my heart to thee, heroic land—
> To thee or in thy morning when the Sun
> Flashed on thy giant limbs—thy lurid noon—
> Or in thy depth of night, fierce-thoughted one—
> Wrestling with phantoms of thy own wild soul,
> Or, stone-still, silent, waiting for the dawn,
> I give my heart to thee, heroic land.
>
> I give my heart to thee, ideal land,
> Far-soaring sister of the starry throng.
> O fleet of wing, what journeyings are thine,

What goal, what god attracts thee? What unseen
Glory reflected makes thy face a flame?
Leave me not; where thou goest, let me go.
I give my heart to thee, ideal land.

ANONYMOUS

THE MAN FROM THE NORTH COUNTRIE

He came from the North, and his words were few,
But his voice was kind, and his heart was true,
And I knew by his eyes no guile had he,
So I married the man of the North Countrie.

Oh, Garryowen may be more gay,
Than this quiet street of Ballibay;
And I know the sun shines softly down
On the river that passes my native town.

But there's not—I say it with joy and pride—
Better man than mine in Munster wide;
And Limerick Town has no happier hearth,
Than mine has been with my man of the North.

I wish that in Munster they only knew
The kind, kind neighbours I came unto;
Small hate or scorn would ever be
Between the South and the North Countrie.

THE PEOPLE

Other races are said to have preceded the Celts in Ireland. Danes, Saxons, Normans, Scots, and English have long since blended with the Celts and their predecessors to form a people with distinctive faults and virtues. As the following selections will show, the poets are inclined to sing the virtues. And Irish who are not poets are similarly addicted.

Richard Brinsley Sheridan was born in Dublin in 1751, but his family moved to England while he was still a boy and he was educated at Harrow. He married an English girl and three of his granddaughters married into great English families. One became Dutchess of Somerset, another Lady Stirling-Maxwell, another Countess of Dufferin. The son of the Countess, Lord Dufferin, great-grandson of Sheridan, held many important offices in the Empire, including Governor-General of Canada. He retired from this post to become British Ambassador to Russia. To a distinguished Canadian audience assembled in 1878 to welcome his successor, Lord Lorne, he followed praise of His Lordship with these words:

And yet, alas! gentlemen, pleasant and agreeable as is the prospect for you and them, we must acknowledge there is one drawback to the picture. Lord Lorne has, as I have said, a multitude of merits, but even spots will be discovered on the sun, and unfortunately an irreparable, *and, as I may call it, a congenital defect attaches to his appointment. Lord Lorne is not an Irishman! It is not his fault—he did the best he could for himself—he came as near the right thing as possible by being born a Celtic Highlander.*

There is no doubt the world is best administered by Irishmen. Things never went better with us either at home or abroad than when Lord Palmerston ruled Great Britain—Lord Mayo governed India—Lord Monck directed the destinies of Canada—and the Robinsons, the Kennedys, the Laffans, the Callaghans, the Gores, the Hennesys, administered the affairs of our Australian colonies and West Indian possessions. Have not even the French at last made the same discovery in the person of Marshall MacMahon? But still we must be generous, and it is right Scotchmen should have a turn. After all, Scotland only got her name because she was conquered by the Irish—and if the real truth were known, it is probable the house of Invernary owes most of its glory to an Irish origin.

Nay, I will go a step further—I would even let the poor Englishman take an occasional turn at the helm—if for no better reason than to make him aware how much better we manage the business. But you have not come to that yet, and though you have been spoiled by having been given three Irish governor-generals in succession, I am sure you will find that your new viceroy's personal and acquired qualifications will more than counterbalance his ethnological disadvantages.

The pride of this English nobleman in his trace of Irish ancestry may throw some light on why we Irish are so Irish—and so do the verses that follow.

THE IRISHMAN

James Orr (1770-1816) was a Protestant Ulsterman who fought at Antrim in the rebellion of 1798. He is famous principally for the following verses:

The savage loves his native shore,
　　Though rude the soil and chill the air;
Then well may Erin's sons adore
　　Their isle which nature formed so fair.
What flood reflects a shore so sweet
　　As Shannon great, or pastoral Bann?
Or who a friend or foe can meet
　　So generous as an Irishman?

His hand is rash, his heart is warm,
　　But honesty is still his guide;
None more repents a deed of harm,
　　And none forgives with nobler pride;
He may be duped, but won't be dared—
　　More fit to practice than to plan;
He dearly earns his poor reward,
　　And spends it like an Irishman.

If strange or poor, for you he'll pay,
　　And guide to where you safe may be;
If you're his guest, while e'er you stay,
　　His cottage holds a jubilee.
His inmost soul he will unlock,
　　And if he may your secrets scan,
Your confidence he scorns to mock,
　　For faithful is an Irishman.

By honor bound in woe or weal,
　　Whate'er she bids he dares to do;
Try him with bribes—they won't prevail;

Prove him in fire—you'll find him true.
He seeks not safety, let his post
  Be where it ought in danger's van;
And if the field of fame be lost,
  It won't be by an Irishman.

These verses contradict the statement which Boswell attributes to Dr. Samuel Johnson:

> *"The Irish are not in a conspiracy to cheat the world by false representations of their countrymen. No sir; the Irish are a fair people—they never speak well of one another."*

John Payne, an English traveler in Ireland in 1589, wrote: "Their entertainment for your diet shall be more welcome and plentiful than cleanly and handsome; for although they never did see you before they will make you the best chear their country yeeldeth for two or three daies, and take not anything therefore."

Almost a hundred years later, Arthur Young filled two volumes with the report of his tours of Ireland in 1776, 1777, and 1778. He wrote: "The circumstances which struck me most in the common Irish were vivacity and a great and eloquent volubility in speech. They are infinitely more chearful and lively than anything we commonly see in England, having nothing of that incivility of sullen silence, with which so many enlightened Englishmen seem to wrap themselves up, as if retiring within their own importance. Their love of society is as remarkable as their curiosity is insatiable; and their hospitality to all comers, be their own poverty ever so pinching, has too much merit to be forgotten."

FRANCIS A. FAHY (1854- ?)

THE DONOVANS

If you would like to see the height of hospitality,
The cream of kindly welcome, and the core of cordiality:
Joys of all the olden time—you're wishing to recall again?
Come down to Donovans, and there you'll meet them all
     again.

Céad míle fáilte [1] they'll give you down at Donovans,
As cheery as the springtime and Irish as the
     cannawaun [2]
The wish of my heart is, if ever I had any one—
That every luck that lightens life may light upon the
     Donovans.

As soon as e'er you lift the latch, the little ones are
     meeting you;
Soon as you're beneath the thatch, oh! kindly looks are
     greeting you:
Scarcely are you ready to be holding out the fist to them,
When down by the fireside you're sitting in the midst
     of them.

There sits the cailín deas [3]—oh! where on earth's the
     peer of her?
The modest face, the gentle grace, the humor and the
     cheer of her—
Eyes like the summer skies when twin stars beam above
     in them,
Oh! proud will be the boy that's to light the lamp of love
     in them.

Then when you rise to go, it's "Ah, then, now sit down
     again!"

---

[1] Céad míle fáilte: a hundred thousand welcomes.
[2] Cannawaun: bog-cotton.
[3] Cailín deas: pretty girl.

"Isn't it the haste you're in?" and "Won't you soon come
  round again?"
Your *caubeen* and your overcoat you'd better put astray
  from them,
'T will take you all your time to try and tear yourself
  away from them.

Céad míle fáilte they'll give you down at Donovans,
As cheery as the springtime and Irish as the *cannawaun*
The wish of my heart is, if ever I had any one—
That every luck that lightens life may light upon the
  Donovans.

JAMES CLARENCE MANGAN

Translated from the Gaelic

THE WOMAN OF THREE COWS

*"The Woman of Three Cows" is not necessarily Irish. We meet
her in the United States—sometimes with three Cadillacs.*

O Woman of Three Cows, *agra!* don't let your tongue
  thus rattle!
Oh, don't be saucy, don't be stiff, because you may have
  cattle.
I have seen—and here's my hand to you, I only say
  what's true—
A many a one with twice your stock not half so proud
  as you.

Good luck to you, don't scorn the poor, and don't be
  their despiser;
For worldly wealth soon melts away, and cheats the very
  miser;
And death soon strips the proudest wreath from haughty

54

human brows—
Then don't be stiff, and don't be proud, good Woman of
    Three Cows.

See where Momonia's heroes lie, proud Owen Mor's
    descendants,
'Tis they that won the glorious name, and had the grand
    attendants;
If they were forced to bow to Fate, as every mortal bows,
Can you be proud, can you be stiff, my Woman of
    Three Cows?

The brave sons of the Lord of Clare, they left the land to
    mourning;
Mavrone! For they were banished, with no hope of their
    returning.
Who knows in what abodes of want those youths were
    driven to house?
Yet you can give yourself these airs, O Woman of
    Three Cows.

Oh, think of Donnel of the Ships, the Chief whom
    nothing daunted,
See how he fell in distant Spain unchronicled, unchanted;
He sleeps, the great O'Sullivan, where thunder cannot
    rouse—
Then ask yourself, should you be proud, good Woman of
    Three Cows?

O'Ruark, Maguire, those souls of fire, whose names are
    shrined in story:
Think how their great achievements once made Erin's
    greatest glory.
Yet now their bones lie mouldering under weeds and
    cypress boughs—
And so, for all your pride, will yours, O Woman of
    Three Cows.

Th' O'Carrols, also, famed when fame was only for the
    boldest,
Rest in forgotten sepulchres with Erin's best and oldest;
Yet who so great as they of yore in battle or carouse?
Just think of that, and hide your head, good Woman of
    Three Cows.

Your neighbor's poor; and you, it seems, are big with
    vain ideas,
Because, *inagh!* you've got three cows—one more, I see,
    than she has;
That tongue of yours wags more at times than charity
    allows;
But if you're strong be merciful—great Woman of
    Three Cows.

AVRAN

Now, there you go; you still, of course, keep up your
    scornful bearing,
And I'm too poor to hinder you; but by the cloak I'm
    wearing,
If I had but four cows myself, even though you were my
    spouse,
I'd thwack you well, to cure your pride, my Woman of
    Three Cows.

C. J. BOLAND

THE TWO TRAVELERS

*No other Irishman equals Frederick Boland in international
recognition. This cosmopolitan personage, as president of the
United Nations, headed a group of one hundred countries. His
uncle, C. J. Boland, at the other extreme, concentrated his
talents on writing many poems about one of Ireland's thirty-*

56

two counties. One of these poems, "The Two Travelers," is a delightful glorification of parochialism. All the places named by the second traveler are in the County Tipperary.

"All over the world," the traveler said,
    "In my peregrinations I've been;
And there's nothing remarkable, living or dead,
    But these eyes of mine have seen—
From the lands of the ape and marmozet,
    To the lands of the Fellaheen."
Said the other, "I'll lay you an even bet
    You were never in Farranalleen."

"I've hunted in woods near Seringapatam,
    And sailed in the polar seas.
I fished for a week in the Gulf of Siam
    And lunched on the Chersonese.
I've lived in the valleys of fair Cashmere,
    Under Himalay's snowy ridge."
Then the other impatiently said, "See here,
    Were you ever at Laffan's Bridge?"

"I've lived in the land where tobacco is grown,
    In the suburbs of Santiago;
And I spent two years in Sierra Leone,
    And one in Del Fuego.
I walked across Panama all in a day,
    Ah me! but the road was rocky."
The other replied, "Will you kindly say,
    Were you ever at Horse-and-Jockey?"

"I've borne my part in a savage fray,
    When I got this wound from a Lascar;
We were bound just then from Mandalay
    For the island of Madagascar.
Ah! the sun never tired of shining there,
    And the trees canaries sang in."

"What of that?" said the other, "sure, I've a pair,
   And there's lots of them over in Drangan."

"I've hunted the tigers in Turkestan,
   In Australia the kangaroos;
And I lived six months as a medicine man
   To a tribe of the Katmandoos.
And I've stood on the scene of Olympic games,
   Where the Grecians showed their paces."
The other asked, "Now tell me James,
   Were you ever at Fethard Races?"

"Don't talk of your hunting in Yucatan,
   Or your fishing off St. Helena;
I'd rather see young fellows hunting the "wren"
   In the hedges of Tubberaheena.
No doubt the scenes of a Swiss canton
   Have a passable sort of charm,
Give me a sunset on Slievenamon
   From the road at Hackett's farm.

"And I'd rather be strolling along the quay,
   And watching the river flow,
Than growing tea with the cute Chinee,
   Or mining in Mexico.
And I wouldn't care much for Sierra Leone,
   If I hadn't seen Killenaule,
And the man that was never in Mullinahone
   Shouldn't say he had traveled at all."

*Since my Cleary ancestors came from Mullinahone, I must agree
with Mr. Boland's conclusion.*

When schools were finally introduced into Ireland and Catholic children were permitted access to reading, writing, and arithmetic, every schoolroom was obliged to display this charming verse:

> I thank the goodness and the grace
> That on my birth have smiled
> And made me in these Christian days
> A happy English child.

PADRAIC COLUM

A POOR SCHOLAR OF THE 'FORTIES

Padraic Colum, born in 1881, wrote plays for the Abbey Theater before coming to the United States. He has written many books and has served as president of the Poetry Society of America.

My eyelids red and heavy are
With bending o'er the smold'ring peat.
I know the Aeneid now by heart,
My Virgil read in cold and heat,
In loneliness and hunger smart.
   And I know Homer, too, I ween,
   As Munster poets know Ossian.

And I must walk this road that winds
'Twixt bog and bog, while east there lies
A city with its men and books;
With treasures open to the wise,
Heart-words from equals, comrade-looks;
   Down here they have but tale and song,
   They talk Repeal the whole night long.

"You teach Greek verbs and Latin nouns,"
The dreamer of Young Ireland said,
"You do not hear the muffled call,
The sword being forged, the far-off tread
Of hosts to meet as Gael and Gall—
    What good to us your wisdom-store,
    Your Latin verse, your Grecian lore?"

And what to me is Gael or Gall?
Less than the Latin or the Greek—
I teach these by the dim rush-light
In smoky cabins night and week.
But what avail my teaching slight?
    Years hence, in rustic speech, a phrase,
    As in wild earth a Grecian vase!

PADRAIC COLUM

AN OLD WOMAN OF THE ROADS

O, to have a little house!
To own the hearth and stool and all!
The heaped-up sods upon the fire,
The pile of turf against the wall!

To have a clock with weights and chains
And pendulum swinging up and down!
A dresser filled with shining delph,
Speckled and white and blue and brown!

I could be busy all the day
Clearing and sweeping hearth and floor,
And fixing on their shelf again
My white and blue and speckled store!

I could be quiet there at night

Beside the fire and by myself,
Sure of a bed, and loath to leave
The ticking clock and the shining delph!

Och! but I'm weary of mist and dark,
The roads where there's never a house or bush,
And tired I am of bog and road,
And the crying wind and the lonesome hush!

And I am praying to God on high,
And I am praying Him night and day,
For a little house—a house of my own—
Out of the wind's and the rain's way.

THOMAS MACDONAGH

JOHN-JOHN

Thomas MacDonagh (1878-1916), the author of this poem, was shot by the British as one of the leaders of the rising of Easter Week.

I dreamt last night of you, John-John,
    And thought you called to me;
And when I woke this morning, John,
    Yourself I hoped to see;
But I was all alone, John-John,
    Though still I heard your call:
I put my boots and bonnet on,
    And took my Sunday shawl,
And went, full sure to find you, John,
                To Nenagh fair.

The fair was just the same as then,
    Five years ago to-day,
When first you left the thimble men

And came with me away;
For there again were thimble men
    And shooting galleries,
And card-trick men and Maggie men
    Of all sorts and degrees—
But not a sight of you, John-John,
            Was anywhere.

I turned my face to home again,
    And called myself a fool
To think you'd leave the thimble men
    And live again by rule,
And go to mass and keep the fast
    And till the little patch:
My wish to have you home was past
    Before I raised the latch
And pushed the door and saw you, John,
            Sitting down there.

How cool you came in here, begad,
    As if you owned the place!
But rest yourself there now, my lad,
    'Tis good to see your face;
My dream is out, and now by it
    I think I know my mind:
At six o'clock this house you'll quit,
    And leave no grief behind;—
But until six o'clock, John-John,
            My bit you'll share.

My neighbours' shame of me began
    When first I brought you in;
To wed and keep a tinker man
    They thought a kind of sin;
But now this three year since you're gone
    'Tis pity me they do,
And that I'd rather have John-John,
    Than that they'd pity you.

Pity for me and you, John-John,
    I could not bear.

Oh, you're my husband right enough,
    But what's the good of that?
You know you never were the stuff
    To be the cottage cat,
To watch the fire and hear me lock
    The door and put out Shep—
But there now, it is six o'clock
    And time for you to step.
God bless and keep you far, John-John!
    And that's my prayer.

Arthur Young, in his volumes reporting his visits to every part of Ireland in 1776, 1777, and 1778, had the following comments on dancing and education:

All the poor people, both men and women, learn to dance, and are exceedingly fond of the amusement. A ragged lad, without shoes or stockings, has been seen in a mud barn, leading a girl in the same trim for a minuet.

Weddings are always celebrated with much dancing; and a Sunday rarely passes without a dance; there are few among them who will not, after a hard day's work, gladly walk seven miles to have a dance.

Dancing-masters of their own rank travel through the country from cabbin to cabbin, with a piper or blind fiddler; and the pay is six pence a quarter. Other branches of education are likewise much attended to, every child of the poorest family learning to read, write, and cast accounts.

JAMES LYMAN MOLLOY (1837-1909)

THE KERRY DANCE

O, the days of the Kerry dancing, O, the ring of the
      piper's tune!
O, for one of those hours of gladness, gone, alas! like
      our youth too soon;
When the boys began to gather in the glen of a summer
      night,
And the Kerry piper's tuning made us long with wild
      delight,
Oh, to think of it; O, to dream of it, fills my heart with
      tears.

Was there ever a sweeter colleen in the dance than
      Eily Moore?
Or a prouder lad than Thady, as he boldly took the
      floor?
"Lads and lasses to your places; up the middle and down
      again."
Ah! the merry hearted laughter ringing through the
      happy glen!
O, to think of it, O, to dream of it, fills my heart with
      tears!

Time goes on and the happy years are dead,
And one by one the merry hearts are fled;
Silent now is the wild and lonely glen,
Where the bright glad laugh will echo ne'er again,
Only dreaming of days gone by, fills my heart with tears!

Loving voices of old companions, stealing out of the
      past once more,
And the sound of the dear old music, soft and sweet as
      in days of yore,
When the boys began to gather in the glen of a summer
      night,

And the Kerry piper's tuning made us long with wild
    delight,
O, to think of it, O, to dream of it, fills my heart with
    tears!

O, the days of the Kerry dancing, O, the ring of the
    piper's tune!
O, for one of those hours of gladness, gone, alas! like our
    youth too soon.

PATRICK J. McCALL (1861- ?)

HERSELF AND MYSELF

An Old Man's Song

'Twas beyond at Macreddin, at Owen Doyle's weddin',
    The boys got the pair of us out for a reel.
Says I: "Boys, excuse us." Says they: "Don't refuse us."
    "I'll play nice and aisy," says Larry O'Neil.
So off we went trippin' it, up an' down steppin' it—
    Herself and Myself on the back of the doore;
Till Molly—God bless her!—fell into the dresser,
    An' I tumbled over a child on the floore.

Says Herself to Myself: "We're as good as the best of
    them."
    Says Myself to Herself: "Sure, we're betther than gold."
Says Herself to Myself: "We're as young as the rest
    o'them."
    Says Myself to Herself: "Troth, we'll never grow old."

As down the lane goin', I felt my heart growin'
    As young as it was forty-five years ago.
'Twas here in this *bóreen* I first kissed my *stóireen*—
    A sweet little colleen with skin like the snow.
I looked at my woman—a song she was hummin'

65

As old as the hills, so I gave her a *pogue;*
'Twas like our old courtin', half sarious, half sportin',
  When Molly was young, an' when hoops were in
      vogue.

When she'd say to Myself: "You can court with the
      best o' them."
  When I'd say to Herself: "Sure, I'm betther than
      gold."
When she'd say to Myself: "You're as wild as the rest
      o' them."
  And I'd say to Herself: "Troth, I'm time enough old."

THOMAS MOORE

COME, SEND 'ROUND THE WINE

Come, send 'round the wine, and leave points of belief
  To simpleton sages and reasoning fools;
This moment's a flower too fair and brief
  To be wither'd and stain'd by the dust of the schools.
Your glass may be purple, and mine may be blue,
  But while they're fill'd from the same bright bowl,
The fool that would quarrel for difference of hue
  Deserves not the comfort they shed o'er the soul.

Shall I ask the brave soldier who fights by my side
  In the cause of mankind, if our creeds agree?
Shall I give up the friend I have valued and tried,
  If he kneel not before the same altar with me?
From the heretic girl of my soul should I fly,
  To seek somewhere else a more orthodox kiss?
No, perish the hearts, and the laws that try
  Truth, valor, or love, by a standard like this!

66

GERALD, EARL OF DESMOND

AGAINST BLAME OF WOMEN

*These verses by Gerald, Earl of Desmond, were written about
1398 and were translated from the Gaelic by the Earl of Longford about forty years ago. The Earl of Longford, nephew of
Lord Dunsany, managed the Gate Theater in Dublin, wrote several plays, and published three volumes of translations.*

Speak not ill of womankind,
    'Tis no wisdom if you do.
You that fault in women find,
    I would not be praised of you.

Sweetly speaking, witty, clear,
    Tribe most lovely to my mind,
Blame of such I hate to hear.
    Speak not ill of womankind.

Bloody treason, murderous act,
    Not by women were designed,
Bells o'erthrown nor churches sacked,
    Speak not ill of womankind.

Bishop, King upon his throne,
    Primate skilled to loose and bind,
Sprung of women every one!
    Speak not ill of womankind.

For a brave young fellow long
    Hearts of women oft have pined.
Who would dare their love to wrong?
    Speak not ill of womankind.

Paunchy greybeards never more
    Hope to please a woman's mind.
Poor young chieftains they adore!
    Speak not ill of womankind.

JOHN BOYLE O'REILLY

THE CRY OF THE DREAMER

John Boyle O'Reilly (1844-1890) enlisted in the British army, preached Fenianism, and won adherents until he was convicted of treason-felony and transported to Australia. He escaped to the United States where he founded the Boston Pilot *and became a distinguished journalist and author.*

I am tired of planning and toiling
In the crowded hives of men;
Heart-weary of building and spoiling
And spoiling and building again.
And I long for the dear old river,
Where I dreamed my youth away;
For a dreamer lives forever,
And a toiler dies in a day.

I am sick of the showy seeming
Of a life that is half a lie;
Of the faces lined with scheming
In the throng that hurries by.
From the sleepless thoughts' endeavour,
I would go where the children play;
For a dreamer lives forever,
And a thinker dies in a day.

I can feel no pride but pity
For the burdens the rich endure;
There is nothing sweet in the city
But the patient lives of the poor.
Ah, the little hands too skillful,
And the child-mind choked with weeds!
The daughter's heart grown willful,
And the father's heart that bleeds!

No, No! from the street's rude bustle,

From trophies of mart and stage,
I would fly to the woods' low rustle
And the meadows' kindly page.
Let me dream as of old by the river,
And be loved for the dream alway;
For a dreamer lives forever,
And a toiler dies in a day.

STOPFORD A. BROOKE

THE EARTH AND MAN

Stopford A. Brooke (1832-1916) wrote books of poetry and of theology. He left the ministry of the Church of England to become a Unitarian. With T. W. H. Rolleston he edited an anthology of Irish poetry in 1909.

A little sun, a little rain,
  A soft wind blowing from the west,
And woods and fields are sweet again,
  And warmth within the mountain's breast.

So simple is the earth we tread,
  So quick with love and life her frame,
Ten thousand years have dawned and fled,
  And still her magic is the same.

A little love, a little trust,
  A soft impulse, a sudden dream,
And life as dry as desert dust
  Is fresher than a mountain stream.

So simple is the heart of man,
  So ready for new hope and joy;
Ten thousand years since it began
  Have left it younger than a boy.

THE CLERGY

Touching pictures of the Irish priest are found in "The Ballad of Father Gilligan" by William Butler Yeats and in "Soggarth Aroon" by John Banim, but the most-loved verses on the subject are "Father O'Flynn" by Alfred Perceval Graves. These poems show why the conquering English were never able to destroy the fierce loyalty of the Irish to their priests.

ALFRED PERCEVAL GRAVES

FATHER O'FLYNN

Alfred Perceval Graves (1846-1931) was the son of the Protestant Bishop of Limerick. He was Inspector of Schools of Ireland for thirty-five years and produced several volumes of songs and poems. He was president of the Irish Literary Society.

Of priests we can offer a charmin' variety,
Far renowned for larnin' and piety;
Still, I'd advance ye widout impropriety,
Father O'Flynn is the flower of them all.

Here's a health to you, Father O'Flynn,
Slainte, and *slainte,* and *slainte* agin;

70

      Powerfulest preacher, and
      Tinderest teacher, and
   Kindliest creature in ould Donegal.

Don't talk of your Provost and Fellows of Trinity,
Famous forever at Greek and Latinity,
Dad and the divels and all at Divinity,
   Father O'Flynn'd make hares of them all.
    Come, I vinture to give you my word,
    Never the likes of his logic was heard,
      Down from Mythology
      Into Thayology,
Troth! and Concology if he'd the call.

Och! Father O'Flynn you've the wonderful way wid you,
All ould sinners are wishful to pray wid you,
And the young childer are wild for to play wid you,
   You've such a way wid you, Father avick!
    Still for all you've so gentle a soul,
    Gad, you've your flock in the grandest control;
      Checking the crazy ones,
      Coaxin' onaisy ones,
Liftin' the lazy ones on wid the stick.

And though quite avoidin' all foolish frivolity,
Still at all seasons of innocent jollity,
Where was the play-boy could claim an equality
   At comicality, Father, wid you?
    Once the Bishop looked grave at your jest,
    Till this remark set him off wid the rest:
      "Is it lave gaiety
      All to the laity?
Cannot the clargy be Irishmen too?"

      Here's a health to you, Father O'Flynn,
     Slainte, and *slainte,* and *slainte* agin;
      Powerfulest preacher, and

Tinderest teacher, and
Kindliest creature in ould Donegal.

JOHN BANIM

SOGGARTH AROON

*When only ten years old John Banim (1798-1844) had written
a romance and some poetry. He entered college at thirteen. On
graduation he became an artist and teacher of drawing. His
play, "Damon and Pythias," was a success in London in 1821.
With his brother Michael he wrote the popular* Tales by the
O'Hara Family.

Am I the slave they say,
  Soggarth Aroon? *
Since you did show the way,
  Soggarth Aroon,
Their slave no more to be,
While they would work with me
Ould Ireland's slavery,
  Soggarth Aroon!

Loyal and brave to you,
  Soggarth Aroon,
Yet be no slave to you,
  Soggarth Aroon,—
Nor, out of fear to you—
Stand up so near to you—
Och! out of fear to *you!*
  Soggarth Aroon!

Who, in the winter's night,
  Soggarth Aroon,
When the cold blast did bite,

---

* *Soggarth Aroon:* Priest dear.

72

Soggarth Aroon,
Came to my cabin-door,
And, on my earthen-floor,
Knelt by me, sick and poor,
    Soggarth Aroon?

Who, on the marriage-day,
    Soggarth Aroon,
Made the poor cabin gay,
    Soggarth Aroon—
And did both laugh and sing
Making our hearts to ring,
At the poor christening,
    Soggarth Aroon?

Who, as friend only met,
    Soggarth Aroon,
Never did flout me yet,
    Soggarth Aroon?
And when my hearth was dim,
Gave, while his eye did brim,
What I should give to him,
    Soggarth Aroon?

Och! you, and only you,
    Soggarth Aroon!
And for this I was true to you,
    Soggarth Aroon;
In love they'll never shake,
When for ould Ireland's sake,
We a true part did take,
    Soggarth Aroon!

THE BALLAD OF FATHER GILLIGAN

The old priest, Peter Gilligan,
Was weary night and day;
For half his flock were in their beds,
Or under green sods lay.

Once, while he nodded on a chair,
At the moth-hour of eve,
Another poor man sent for him,
And he began to grieve.

"I have no rest, nor joy, nor peace,
For people die and die";
And after cried he, "God forgive!
My body spake, not I!"

And then, half lying on the chair
He knelt, prayed, fell asleep,
And the moth-hour went from the fields,
And stars began to peep.

They slowly into millions grew,
And leaves shook in the wind,
And God covered the world with shade,
And whispered to mankind.

Upon the time of sparrow chirp
When the moths came once more,
The old priest, Peter Gilligan,
Stood upright on the floor.

"Mavrone, mavrone! the man has died,
While I slept on the chair."
He roused his horse out of its sleep,
And rode with little care.

He rode now as he never rode,
By rocky lane and fen;
The sick man's wife opened the door:
"Father! you come again."

"And is the poor man dead?" he cried.
"He died an hour ago."
The old priest, Peter Gilligan,
In grief swayed to and fro.

"When you were gone, he turned and died
As merry as a bird."
The old priest, Peter Gilligan,
He knelt him at that word.

"He who hath made the night of stars
For souls who tire and bleed,
Sent one of His great angels down
To help me in my need.

"He who is wrapped in purple robes,
With planets in His care,
Had pity on the least of things
Asleep upon a chair."

GERALD GRIFFIN

THE SISTER OF CHARITY

Gerald Griffin (1903-1940) was born in Limerick, worked as a journalist in London, and wrote plays and novels. He later became a Christian Brother and spent his final years teaching the poor.

She once was a lady of honor and wealth,
Bright glow'd on her features the roses of health;

Her vesture was blended of silk and of gold,
And her motion shook perfume from every fold:
Joy revell'd around her—love shone at her side,
And gay was her smile, as the glance of a bride;
And light was her step in the mirth-sounding hall,
When she heard of the daughters of Vincent de Paul.

She felt, in her spirit, the summons of grace,
That call'd her to live for the suffering race;
And heedless of pleasure, of comfort, of home,
Rose quickly like Mary, and answered, "I come."
She put from her person the trappings of pride,
And pass'd from her home, with the joy of a bride,
Nor wept at the threshold, as onwards she moved—
For her heart was on fire in the cause it approved.

. . .

Those feet, that to music could gracefully move,
Now bear her alone on the mission of love;
Those hands that once dangled the perfume and gem
Are tending the helpless, or lifted for them;
That voice that once echo'd the song of the vain,
Now whispers relief to the bosom of pain;
And the hair that was shining with diamond and pearl,
Is wet with the tears of the penitent girl.

Her down-bed a pallet—her trinkets a bead,
Her lustre—one taper that serves her to read;
Her sculpture—the crucifix nail'd by her bed;
Her paintings one print of the thorn-crowned head;
Her cushion—the pavement that wearies her knees;
Her music the psalm, or the sigh of disease;
The delicate lady lives mortified there,
And the feast is forsaken for fasting and prayer.

. . .

Unshrinking where pestilence scatters his breath,
Like an angel she moves, 'mid the vapor of death;
Where rings the loud musket, and flashes the sword,
Unfearing she walks, for she follows the Lord.
How sweetly she bends o'er each plague-tainted face
With looks that are lighted with holiest grace;
How kindly she dresses each suffering limb,
For she sees in the wounded the image of Him.

Behold her, ye worldly! behold her, ye vain!
Who shrink from the pathway of virtue and pain;
Who yield up to pleasure your nights and your days,
Forgetful of service, forgetful of praise.
Ye lazy philosophers—self-seeking men,—
Ye fireside philanthropists, great at the pen,
How stands in the balance your eloquence weighed
With the life and the deeds of that high-born maid?

ELLEN MARY PATRICK DOWNING

THE OLD CHURCH AT LISMORE

*Ellen Mary Patrick Downing (1828-1869) wrote much patriotic
verse which appeared in* The Nation *under the name Mary.
Later, as a nun, she took the name Sister Mary Alphonsus. In
telling of his tour of Ireland in 1842, William M. Thackeray
refers to:*

*The graceful spire of Lismore church, the prettiest I
have ever seen in, or, I think, out of Ireland. Nor in any
country that I have visited have I seen a view more
noble. In the old graveyard Protestants and Catholics lie
together—that is not together; for each has a side of the
ground where they sleep, and, so occupied, do not
quarrel.*

Old Church, thou still art Catholic!—e'en dream they as
    they may
That the new rites and worship have swept the old away;
There is no form of beauty raised by Nature, or by art,
That preaches not God's saving truths to man's adoring
    heart!

In vain they tore the altar down; in vain they flung aside
The mournful emblem of the death which our sweet
    Saviour died;
In vain they left no single trace of saint or angel here—
Still angel-spirits haunt the ground, and to the soul
    appear.

I marvel how, in scenes like these, so coldly they can
    pray,
Nor hold sweet commune with the dead who once knelt
    down as they;
Yet not as they, in sad mistrust or sceptic doubt—for, oh,
They looked in hope to the blessed saints, these dead of
    long ago.

And, then, the churchyard, soft and calm, spread out
    beyond the scene
With sunshine warm and soothing shade and trees upon
    its green;
Ah! though their cruel Church forbid, are there no
    hearts will pray
For the poor souls that trembling left that cold and
    speechless clay?

My God! I am a Catholic! I grew into the ways
Of my dear Church since first my voice could lisp a
    word of praise;
But oft I think though my first youth were taught and
    trained awrong,
I still had learnt the one true faith from Nature and
    from song!

For still, whenever dear friends die, it is such joy to
  know
They are not all beyond the care that healed their
  wounds below,
That we can pray them into peace, and speed them to
  the shore
Where clouds and cares and thorny griefs shall vex their
  hearts no more.

And the sweet saints, so meek below, so merciful above:
And the pure angels, watching still with such untiring
  love:
And the kind Virgin, Queen of Heaven, with all her
  mother's care,
Who prays for earth, because she knows what breaking
  hearts are there!

Oh, let us lose no single link that our dear Church has
  bound,
To keep our hearts more close to Heaven, on earth's
  ungenial ground;
But trust in saint and martyr yet, and o'er their hallowed
  clay,
Long after we have ceased to weep, kneel faithful down
  to pray.

So shall the land for us be still the Sainted Isle of old,
Where hymn and incense rise to Heaven, and holy beads
  are told;
And even the ground they tore from God, in years of
  crime and woe,
Instinctive with His truth and love, shall breathe of
  long ago!

George Berkley, Bishop of Cloyne (1684-1753), was called by
Thomas Huxley "one of the noblest and purest figures of his

time," and was similarly lauded by Pope and Swift. He once visited Rhode Island to promote his plan for the evangelization of the American Indians. Most widely quoted has been the final verse of his poem entitled "On the Prospect of Planting Arts and Learning in America":

> Westward the course of empire takes its way,
> The first four acts already past;
> A fifth shall close the drama with the day—
> Time's noblest offspring is the last.

Bishop Berkley's three issues of The Querist contained more than eight hundred questions which were influential in inducing Irish gentlemen to organize for the promotion of agriculture, industry, and commerce. Here are a few:

> Whether our Peers and Gentlemen are born Legislators? Or whether that Faculty be acquired by Study and Reflection?

> Whether the Gentleman of Estate hath a right to be idle; and whether he ought not to be the great Promoter and Director of Industry, among his Tenants and Neighbors?

> Whether there be upon Earth any Christian or civilized people so beggarly wretched and destitute as the common Irish? Whether, nevertheless, there is any other people whose wants may be more easily supplied from home?

> Whether an Irish lady, set out with French silks and Flanders lace, may not be said to consume more beef and butter than fifty of our labouring peasants? Whether a woman of fashion ought not to be declared a public enemy?

> Whether there be not every year more Cash circulated

at the Card-Tables of Dublin than at all the Fairs of
Ireland?

Whether all spiritous liquors are not, in truth, Opiates?

Whether the creating of Wants be not the likeliest way
to produce Industry in a People? And whether, if our
Peasants were accustomed to eat Beef and wear Shoes,
they would not be more industrious?

Some of Berkley's questions may have helped to lay the
foundation for the Rebellion of 1798 and those which followed.

Very different from Bishop Berkley was Lord Bristol, Bishop
of Derry, whose arrival at Dublin in 1783 was described as
follows:

He had several carriages to his suite, and sat in an open
landau, drawn by six beautiful horses, caparisoned with
purple ribbons. He was dressed in purple, his horses,
equipages, and servants being in the most splendid trappings and liveries. He had brought to Dublin, as his
escort, a troop of light cavalry; they were splendidly
dressed and accoutred, and were mounted on the finest
chargers that the Bishop or their commander could pro-
cure. A part of these dragoons led the procession, and
another closed it, and some rode on each side of his
Lordship's carriage. Trumpets announced his approach.

Arthur Young reported that in 1778 tithes paid by Catholic
peasants, who lived in poverty, helped to support twenty-two
Protestant bishops in luxury. The bishops also owned hundreds
of thousands of acres of land.

81

LOVE

Two subjects overshadow all others in the poetry of Ireland—
patriotism and affection. For seven centuries the Irish were in
constant vocal, and intermittent physical, rebellion against their
English rulers. Counterbalancing this was pure and beautiful love
for each other, well expressed in song and verse.

Rudyard Kipling put it this way:

For where there are Irish there's loving and fighting,
And when we stop either, it's Ireland no more.

JOHN KEEGAN CASEY

MAIRE MY GIRL

John Keegan Casey (1846-1870), son of a peasant in Westmeath,
wrote his first published poem at the age of sixteen. He was
imprisoned as a Fenian rebel when twenty-one and died before
he reached the age of twenty-four. His funeral was attended by
fifty thousand people. Two volumes of his poems were published, the second while he was in prison.

Over the dim blue hills
Strays a wild river,
Over the dim blue hills
Rests my heart ever.
Dearer and brighter than
Jewels and pearl,
Dwells she in beauty there,
Maire my girl.

Down upon Claris heath
Shines the soft berry,
On the brown harvest tree
Droops the red cherry.
Sweeter thy honey lips,
Softer the curl
Straying adown thy cheeks,
Maire my girl.

'Twas on an April eve
That I first met her;
Many an eve shall pass
Ere I forget her.
Since my young heart has been
Wrapped in a whirl,
Thinking and dreaming of
Maire my girl.

She is too kind and fond
Ever to grieve me,
She has too pure a heart
E'er to deceive me.
Was I Tyrconnell's chief
Or Desmond's earl,
Life would be dark, wanting
Maire my girl.

Over the dim blue hills
Strays a wild river,

Over the dim blue hills
Rests my heart ever;
Dearer and brighter than
Jewels or pearl,
Dwells she in beauty there,
Maire my girl.

MARTIN MACDERMOTT

GIRL OF THE RED MOUTH

*Martin MacDermott (1823-1905) participated in the rebellion
of 1848 and later served as Chief Architect in the Office of Public
Works of the Khedive of Egypt. He supervised the reconstruc-
tion of Alexandria after its bombardment.*

Girl of the red mouth,
  Love me! Love me!
Girl of the red mouth,
    Love me!
'Tis by its curve, I know,
Love fashioneth his bow,
And bends it—ah, even so!
  Oh, girl of the red mouth, love me!

Girl of the blue eye,
  Love me! Love me!
Girl of the dew eye,
    Love me!
Worlds hang for lamps on high;
And thought's world lives in thy
Lustrous and tender eye—
  Oh, girl of the blue eye, love me!

Girl of the swan's neck,
  Love me! Love me!

Girl of the swan's neck,
        Love me!
As a marble Greek doth grow
To his steed's back of snow,
Thy white neck sits thy shoulder so—
    Oh, girl of the swan's neck, love me!

Girl of the low voice,
    Love me! Love me!
Girl of the sweet voice,
        Love me!
Like the echo of a bell—
Like the bubbling of a well—
Sweeter! Love within doth dwell—
    Oh, girl of the low voice, love me!

GERALD GRIFFIN

EILEEN AROON

When, like the early rose,
    Eileen aroon! *
Beauty in childhood blows,
    Eileen aroon!
When, like a diadem,
Buds blush around the stem,
Which is the fairest gem?
    Eileen aroon!

Is it the laughing eye?
    Eileen aroon!
Is it the timid sigh?
    Eileen aroon!
Is it the tender tone,
Soft as the stringed heart's moan?

---

* *Eibhlín a rúin:* Eileen, my treasure.

Oh! it is Truth alone,
Eileen aroon!

When, like the rising day,
Eileen aroon!
Love sends his early ray,
Eileen aroon!
What makes his dawning glow
Changeless through joy or woe?—
Only the constant know,
Eileen aroon!

I know a valley fair,
Eileen aroon!
I knew a cottage there,
Eileen aroon!
Far in that valley's shade
I knew a gentle maid,
Flower of a hazel glade,
Eileen aroon!

Who in the song so sweet?
Eileen aroon!
Who in the dance so fleet?
Eileen aroon!
Dear were her charms to me,
Dearer her laughter free,
Dearest her constancy,
Eileen aroon!

Youth must with time decay,
Eileen aroon!
Beauty must fade away,
Eileen aroon!
Castles are sacked in war,
Chieftains are scattered far,
Truth is a fixed star,
Eileen aroon!

THOMAS OSBORN DAVIS

THE WELCOME

Come in the evening, or come in the morning,
Come when you're looked for, or come without warning,
Kisses and welcome you'll find here before you,
And the oftener you come here the more I'll adore you.
  Light is my heart since the day we were plighted,
  Red is my cheek that they told me was blighted,
  The green of the trees looks far greener than ever,
  And the linnets are singing, "True lovers, don't sever!"

I'll pull you sweet flowers, to wear, if you choose them:
Or, after you've kissed them, they'll lie on my bosom.
I'll fetch from the mountain its breeze to inspire you;
I'll fetch from my fancy a tale that won't tire you.
O your step's like the rain to the summer-vexed farmer,
Or saber and shield to a knight without armor;
  I'll sing you sweet songs till the stars rise above me,
  Then, wandering, I'll wish you, in silence, to love me.

We'll look through the trees at the cliff and the eyrie;
We'll tread round the rath on the track of the fairy;
We'll look on the stars, and we'll list to the river,
Till you'll ask of your darling what gift you can give her.
  O she'll whisper you, "Love as unchangeably beaming,
  And trust, when in secret, most tunefully streaming,
  Till the starlight of heaven above us shall quiver
  As our souls flow in one down eternity's river."

So come in the evening, or come in the morning,
Come when you're looked for, or come without warning,
Kisses and welcome you'll find here before you,
And the oftener you come here the more I'll adore you.

How is it that so many of the poets in this book have English names—Rolleston, Allingham, Todhunter, Davis, Letts, Crawford?

It goes back to a law enacted by the British parliament in 1465, which reads in part as follows:

> *. . . it is ordeyened and established by authority of said parliament that every Irishman that dwells betwixt or amongst Englishmen in the County of Dublin, Myeth, Uriel, or Kildare . . . shall take unto him an English surname on one towne, as Sutton, Chester, Trym, Cork, Kinsale; or colour, as white, black, browne; or arte or science, as smith or carpenter; or office, as cooke, butler; and his issue shall use this name under payne of forfeyting his goods yearely till the premises be done.*

Similar laws followed in later centuries.

Another reason is that men inherited a name from a father and loyalties from a mother. Many centuries ago Queen Elizabeth complained that the Norman nobles in Ireland had become "more Irish than the Irish."

A recent check showed that the most common names in Ireland are: Murphy, Kelly, Sullivan, Walsh, Smith, O'Brien, Byrne, Ryan, Connor, O'Neill, Reilly, Doyle, and Kennedy.

THOMAS OSBORN DAVIS

THE GIRL OF DUNBWY

'Tis pretty to see the girl of Dunbwy
Stepping the mountain statelily—
Though ragged her gown and naked her feet,
No lady in Ireland to match her is meet.

Poor is her diet, and hardly she lies—
Yet a monarch might kneel for a glance of her eyes;
The child of a peasant—yet England's proud Queen
Has less rank in her heart, and less grace in her mien.

Her brow 'neath her raven hair gleams, just as if
A breaker spread white 'neath a shadowy cliff,
And love, and devotion, and energy speak
From her beauty-proud eye, and her passion-pale cheek.

But pale as her cheek is, there's fruit on her lip,
And her teeth flash as white as the crescent moon's tip,
And her form and her step, like the red deer's go past—
As lightsome, as lovely, as haughty, as fast.

I saw her but once, and I looked in her eye,
And she knew that I worshipped in passing her by;
The saint of the wayside—she granted my prayer,
Though we spoke not a word, for her mother was there.

ELLEN MARY PATRICK DOWNING (SISTER MARY ALPHONSUS)

MY OWEN

Proud of you, fond of you, clinging so near to you,
Light is my heart now I know I am dear to you!
Glad is my voice now, so free it may sing for you
All the wild love which is burning within for you!
Tell me once more, tell it over and over,
The tale of that eve which first saw you my lover.
    Now I need never blush
    At my heart's hottest gush—
The wife of my Owen her heart may discover!

Proud of you, fond of you, having all right in you,
Quitting all else through my love and delight in you!
Glad is my heart since 'tis beating so nigh to you!
Light is my step for it always may fly to you!
Clasped in your arms where no sorrow can reach to me,
Reading your eyes till new love they shall teach to me,
    Though wild and weak till now,
    By that blest marriage vow,
More than the wisest know *your* heart shall preach to me.

89

MARY FURLONG

AN IRISH LOVE-SONG

*Mary Furlong (1868-1898) wrote most of her verses between
the ages of fourteen and twenty, after which she devoted herself
to nursing. She died caring for patients in a typhus epidemic.*

I love you, and I love you, and I love you, O my honey!
It isn't for your goodly lands, it isn't for your money;
It isn't for your father's cows, your mother's yellow
      butter,
The love that's in my heart for you no words of mine
      may utter!

The whole world is gone wrong with me since yester-
      morning early,
Above the shoulder of Sliav Ruadh the sun was peeping
      barely,
Your light feet scarcely stirred the dew among the
      scented clover;
O happy dew, O happy grass, those little feet went over!

The breeze had coaxed your nut-brown hair beneath the
      white sun-bonnet,
The sunbeams kissed the corn-flowers blue that you had
      fastened on it,
And danced and danced, and quivered down your gown
      of colored cotton;
And when I looked upon your face I fear I'd quite
      forgotten—

It was not you I came to see this morning but another,
But who could look on that brown head, and ask for
      Tom, the brother?
Your blue eyes have bewitched me quite, the eatin' and
      the dhrinkin'

Have lost the grah* they used to have, of you I'm
    always thinkin'.

The white of wheat is on your cheek, the scarlet of the
    berry
There sweetly blends: on each soft lip the smile comes
    quick and merry;
And oh! the blue, blue eyes that shine beneath their
    silken lashes—
My word! it is for sake of them my bread is turned to
    ashes!

But sure this foolish tongue of mine won't get to tell its
    story—
Oh, how I wish I had the talk of my fine cousin Rory!
Who's just as glib as if he ate the highest English
    Grammar,
And if he loved a thousand times it would not make
    him stammer.

And yet I almost think she cares—for sometimes how
    she blushes!
And so this pleasant eve of May, when all the larks and
    thrushes
Are singing their sweet songs of love, I'll try an' tell my
    story,
Although I cannot sing like them, or speak like cousin
    Rory.

---

* *Grah:* taste.

KITTY NEIL

*John Francis Waller (1810-1894), a graduate of Trinity College
and a member of the Irish bar, wrote five volumes of verse.*

"Ah, sweet Kitty Neil! rise up from your wheel!
    Your neat little foot will be weary from spinning;
Come, trip down with me to the sycamore-tree—
    Half the parish is there, and the dance is beginning.
The sun is gone down, but the full harvest moon
    Shines sweetly and cool on the dew-whiten'd valley,
While all the air rings with the soft, loving things
    Each little bird sings in the green shaded alley."

With a blush and a smile, Kitty rose up the while,
    Her eye in the glass, as she bound her hair, glancing,
'Tis hard to refuse when a young lover sues,
    So she couldn't but choose to—go off to the dancing.
And now on the green the glad groups are seen,
    Each gay-hearted lad with the lass of his choosing;
And Pat, without fail, leads out sweet Kitty Neil—
        Somehow, when he asked, she ne'er thought of
            refusing.

Now Felix Magee puts his pipe to his knee,
    And, with flourish so free, sets each couple in motion;
With a cheer and a bound, the lads patter the ground—
    The maids move around just like swans on the ocean.
Cheeks bright as the rose—feet light as the doe's—
    Now coyly retiring, now boldly advancing;
Search the world all around, from the sky to the ground,
    No such sight can be found as an Irish lass dancing!

Sweet Kate! who could view your bright eyes of deep
        blue

92

Beaming humidly through their dark lashes so
   mildly—
Your fair-turned arm, heaving breast, rounded form—
   Nor feel his heart warm, and his pulses throb wildly?
Poor Pat feels his heart, as he gazes, depart,
   Subdued by the smart of such painful yet sweet love;
The sight leaves his eye as he cries, with a sigh,
   *"Dance light, for my heart it lies under your feet,
      love!"*

LADY MORGAN

KATE KEARNEY

*Lady Morgan (1783-1859) was born Sidney Owenson and wrote
novels, plays, and songs before her marriage to Sir Thomas
Morgan. Her published books, many of them controversial,
totaled more than seventy volumes. Although she moved in
aristocratic British society, she fought vigorously and effectively
to right the wrongs from which her native land suffered.*

O did you not hear of Kate Kearney?
She lives on the banks of Killarney,
From the glance of her eye shun danger and fly,
For fatal's the glance of Kate Kearney!
For that eye is so modestly beaming,
You'd ne'er think of mischief she's dreaming,
Yet oh, I can tell how fatal's the spell
That lurks in the eye of Kate Kearney!

O, should you e'er meet this Kate Kearney,
Who lives on the banks of Killarney,
Beware of her smile, for many a wile
Lies hid in the smile of Kate Kearney.
Though she looks so bewitchingly simple,

There's mischief in every dimple;
Who dares inhale her mouth's spicy gale
Must die by the breath of Kate Kearney.

CHARLES DAWSON SHANLY

KITTY OF COLERAINE

*Charles Dawson Shanly (1811-1875) was born in Dublin, edu-
cated at Trinity College, held official positions in Canada,
worked as a journalist, and wrote books in New York City. He
died in Florida.*

As beautiful Kitty one morning was tripping
    With a pitcher of milk for the fair of Coleraine,
When she saw me she stumbled, the pitcher down
            tumbled,
    And all the sweet buttermilk watered the plain.
"Oh, what shall I do now? 'Twas looking at you now!
    I'm sure such a pitcher I'll ne'er see again.
'Twas the pride of my dairy. Oh, Barney McCleary,
    You're sent as a plague to the girls of Coleraine."

I sat down beside her, and gently did chide her
    That such a misfortune should give her such pain;
A kiss then I gave her, and before I did leave her
    She vowed for such pleasure she'd break it again.
'Twas the haymaking season—I can't tell the reason—
    Misfortunes will never come single, 'tis plain!
For very soon after poor Kitty's disaster
    The devil a pitcher was whole in Coleraine.

ARTHUR STRINGER (1874-1950)

OONAGH OF BALLYBREE

I sailed in me foine new hooker
  To Ballybree, over the bay,
Where Oonagh O'Regan, me ould love,
  Is livin' this many a day.

('Twas Oonagh took up wid a poacher,
  A Ballybree blade called Neal,
Wid niver a ham nor a hare-skin
  But what the poor habbage could steal!)

And Oonagh I found, faith, wid childer
  As thick as the hairs on a goat,
All squealin' and crowdin' like rabbits
  While I showed her me jule av a boat!

"But have ye no wife nor childer?"
  Says she, wid a perk av the head.
(And her bosom as flat as a deck-board,
  And her brats all squealin' for bread!)

"Och, sailin'," says she, "may be sailin',
  But when it's all spoken and done,
'Tis us wid our foine homes and childer
  Are livin' and havin' our fun!"

FRANCIS A. FAHY

THE OLD PLAID SHAWL

Not far from old Kinvara, in the merry month of May,
When birds were singing cheerily, there came across my
  way,

As if from out the sky above an angel chanced to fall,
A little Irish *càilín* in an old plaid shawl.

She tripped along right joyously, a basket on her arm;
And O her face! and O her grace! the soul of saint
  would charm;
Her brown hair rippled o'er her brow, but greatest charm
  of all
Was her modest blue eyes beaming 'neath her old plaid
  shawl.

I courteously saluted her—"God save you, miss," says I;
"God save you kindly, sir," said she, and shyly passed
  me by;
Off went my heart along with her, a captive in her thrall,
Imprisoned in the corner of her old plaid shawl.

Enchanted with her beauty rare, I gazed in pure delight,
Till round an angle of the road she vanished from my
  sight,
But ever since I sighing say, as I that scene recall,
"The grace of God about you and your old plaid shawl."

I've heard of highway robbers that with pistols and with
  knives
Make trembling travellers yield them up their money or
  their lives,
But think of me that handed out my heart and head and
  all
To a simple little *càilín* in an old plaid shawl.

O graceful the mantillas that the signorinas wear,
And tasteful are the bonnets of Parisian ladies fair,
But never cloak, or hood, or robe, in palace, bower, or
  hall,
Clad half such witching beauty as that old plaid shawl.

O some men sigh for riches, and some men live for fame,

And some on history's pages hope to win a glorious name:
My aims are not ambitious, and my wishes are but small—
You might wrap them all together in an old plaid shawl.

WILLIAM PEMBROKE MULCHINOCK

THE ROSE OF TRALEE

William Pembroke Mulchinock (1820-1864) was a prosperous woolen merchant who left Ireland for Boston in 1848. While in America he published a book of verse, of which "The Rose of Tralee" became internationally popular.

The pale moon was rising above the green mountain,
　The sun was declining beneath the blue sea,
When I stray'd with my love to the pure crystal fountain
　That stands in the beautiful vale of Tralee.

She was lovely and fair as the rose of the summer,
　Yet 'twas not her beauty alone that won me,
Oh, no, 'twas the truth in her eyes ever beaming
　That made me love Mary, the Rose of Tralee.

The cool shades of evening their mantle were spreading,
　And Mary, all smiling, was list'ning to me,
The moon through the valley her pale rays were shedding
　When I won the heart of the Rose of Tralee.

Tho' lovely and fair as the rose of the summer,
　Yet 'twas not her beauty alone that won me,
Oh, no, 'twas the truth in her eyes ever beaming
　That made me love Mary, the Rose of Tralee.

LOVELY MARY DONNELLY

Oh, lovely Mary Donnelly, my joy, my only best
If fifty girls were round you, I'd hardly see the rest;
Be what it may the time o' day, the place be where it will
Sweet looks o' Mary Donnelly, they bloom before me still.

Her eyes like mountain water that's flowing on a rock,
How clear they are, how dark they are! they give me
many a shock.
Red rowans warm in sunshine and wetted with a shower,
Could ne'er express the charming lip that has me in its
power.

Her nose is straight and handsome, her eyebrows lifted
up,
Her chin is very neat and pert, and smooth like a china
cup,
Her hair's the brag of Ireland, so weighty and so fine;
It's rolling down upon her neck, and gathered in a twine.

The dance o' last Whit-Monday night exceeded all before,
No pretty girl from miles about was missing from the
floor;
But Mary kept the belt of love, and O but she was gay!
She danced a jig, she sung a song, that took my heart
away.

When she stood up for dancing, her steps were so
complete,
The music nearly killed itself to listen to her feet;
The fiddler mourned his blindness, he heard her so much
praised,
But blessed his luck not to be deaf when once her voice
she raised.

And evermore I'm whistling or lilting what you sung,
Your smile is always in my heart, your name beside my
tongue;
But you've as many sweethearts as you'd count on both
your hands,
And for myself there's not a thumb or little finger stands.

Oh, you're the flower o' womankind in country or in
town;
The higher I exalt you, the lower I'm cast down.
If some great lord should come this way, and see your
beauty bright
And you to be his lady, I'd own it was but right.

Oh, might we live together in a lofty palace hall,
Where joyful music rises, and where scarlet curtains fall!
Oh, might we live together in a cottage mean and small,
With sod or grass the only roof, and mud the only wall!

O lovely Mary Donnelly, your beauty's my distress,
It's far too beauteous to be mine, but I'll never wish it
less.
The proudest place would fit your face, and I am poor
and low
But blessings be about you, dear, wherever you may go.

SAMUEL LOVER

BARNEY O'HEA

*Samuel Lover (1797-1868) was the son of a successful Dublin
businessman from whom he was alienated by his refusal of a
business career. He was first successful as an artist, then as an
author of stories and novels illustrated with his own etchings,
and finally by hundreds of popular songs.*

Now let me alone, though I know you won't,
   Impudent Barney O'Hea!
   It makes me outrageous
   When you're so contagious,
And you'd better look out for the stout Corney Creagh;
   For he is the boy
   That believes I'm his joy,
So you'd better behave yourself, Barney O'Hea!
   Impudent Barney,
   None of your blarney,
   Impudent Barney O'Hea!

I hope you're not going to Bandon Fair,
For indeed I'm not wanting to meet you there,
   Impudent Barney O'Hea!
   For Corney's at Cork,
   And my brother's at work,
And my mother sits spinning at home all the day,
   So no one will be there
   Of poor me to take care,
So I hope you won't follow me, Barney O'Hea!
   Impudent Barney,
   None of your blarney,
   Impudent Barney O'Hea!

But as I was walking up Bandon Street,
Just who do you think that myself should meet,
   But impudent Barney O'Hea!
   He said I looked killin',
   I called him a villain,
And bid him that minute get out of the way;
   He said I was joking
   And grinned so provoking,
I couldn't help laughing at Barney O'Hea!
   Impudent Barney,
   None of your blarney,
   Impudent Barney O'Hea!

He knew 'twas all right when he saw me smile,
For he was the rogue up to ev'ry wile,
    Impudent Barney O'Hea!
    He coaxed me to choose him,
    For if I'd refuse him
He swore he'd kill Corney the very next day;
    So, for fear 'twould go further,
    And just to save murther,
I think I must marry that madcap, O'Hea!
    Bothering Barney,
    'Tis he has the blarney
To make a girl Mistress O'Hea.

SAMUEL LOVER

RORY O'MORE

Young Rory O'More courted Kathleen bawn,
He was bold as a hawk, and she soft as the dawn;
He wished in his heart pretty Kathleen to please,
And he thought the best way to do that was to tease.
"Now, Rory, be aisy," sweet Kathleen would cry,
Reproof on her lips, but a smile in her eye;
"With your tricks I don't know, in troth, what I'm about;
Faith, you've teased till I've put on my cloak inside out."
"Oh! jewel," says Rory, "that same is the way
You've thrated my heart for this many a day,
And 'tis plazed that I am, and why not, to be sure?
For 'tis all for good luck," says bold Rory O'More.

"Indeed, then," says Kathleen, "don't think of the like,
For I half gave a promise to soothering Mike;
The ground that I walk on he loves, I'll be bound."
"Faith," says Rory, "I'd rather love you than the ground."
"Now, Rory, I'll cry, if you don't let me go;
Sure I dream every night that I'm hating you so!"

"Oh!" says Rory, "that same I'm delighted to hear,
For dhrames always go by contrairies, my dear!
Oh! jewel, keep dreaming that same till you die,
And bright morning will give dirty night the black lie;
And 'tis plazed that I am, and why not, to be sure?
Since 'tis all for good luck," says bold Rory O'More.

"Arrah, Kathleen, my darlint, you've teazed me enough,
Sure I've thrashed, for your sake, Dinny Grimes and
         Jim Duff;
And I've made myself, drinking your health, quite a
         baste,
So I think, after that, I may talk to the priest."
Then Rory, the rogue, stole his arm round her neck,
So soft and so white, without freckle or speck,
And he looked in her eyes that were beaming with light,
And he kissed her sweet lips,—don't you think he was
         right?
"Now, Rory, leave off, sir; you'll hug me no more;
That's eight times to-day that you've kissed me before."
"Then here goes another," says he, "to make sure,
For there's luck in odd numbers," said Rory O'More.

SAMUEL LOVER

I'M NOT MYSELF AT ALL!

O I'm not myself at all, Molly dear, Molly dear,
      I'm not myself at all!
Nothin' carin', nothin' knowing, 'tis after you I'm goin',
Faith, your shadow 'tis I'm growin', Molly dear,
      And I'm not myself at all!
Th' other day I went confessin', and I asked the father's
         blessin',
   "But," says I, "don't give me one entirely,
For I fretted so last year but the half of me is here,

102

So give the other half to Molly Brierley."
　　O I'm not myself at all!

O I'm not myself at all, Molly dear, Molly dear,
　　My appetite's so small.
I once could pick a goose, but my buttons is no use,
Faith my tightest coat is loose, Molly dear,
　　And I'm not myself at all!
If thus it is I waste, you'd better, dear, make haste,
　　Before your lover's gone away entirely;
If you don't soon change your mind, not a bit of me
　　　you'll find—
　　And what 'ud you think o' that, Molly Brierley?
　　　O I'm not myself at all!

O my shadow on the wall, Molly dear, Molly dear,
　　Isn't like myself at all.
For I've got so very thin, myself says 'tisn't him,
But that purty girl so slim, Molly dear,
　　And I'm not myself at all!
If thus I smaller grow, all frettin, dear, for you,
　　'Tis you should make me up the deficiency;
So just let Father Taaffe make you my better-half,
　　And you will not the worse of the addition be—
　　　O I'm not myself at all!

I'll be not myself at all, Molly dear, Molly dear,
　　Till you my own I call!
Since a change o'er me there came, sure you might
　　　change your name—
And 'twoud just come to the same, Molly dear,
　　'Twould just come to the same;
For if you and I were one, all confusion would be gone,
　　And 'twould simplify the matter entirely;
And 'twould save us so much bother when we'd both
　　　be one another—
　　So listen now to reason, Molly Brierley.
　　　O I'm not myself at all!

COURTSHIP

I. Under Kitty's Window.

"Ah, then; who is that there talkin'?"
  "Sure it's only me, ye know.
I was thinkin' we'd go walkin'—"
  "Wor ye raly thinkin' so?"

"Och ye needn' be so cruel
  An me thrudged this sivin mile—"
"Is it cruel, Michael, jewel?
  Sure I'm dressin' all the while!"

II. Before Michael's Cottage.

"There now, that's me cottage, Kitty."
  "Is it, Mike?"
"Yis; an' isn't it pretty?"
  "Hm!—lonesome like."

(Lonesome? Now's y'r minute—
  Michael, Strike!)
"Sure if only YOU wor in it—"
  "Arrah, Mike!"

*Although a friend of Robert Emmett and an intensely pa-
triotic Irishman who stood up for his convictions, Thomas Moore
was the darling of British aristocracy. His first book, translations
of sixty-eight odes of the Greek poet Anacreon, published when
Moore was twenty-one years old, was sponsored by the Prince
Regent. At twenty-four he became a British official in Bermuda,
and in 1804 visited Niagara Falls. At a great ball in Dublin
he was so courted and lionized by lords and ladies that his wife*

felt ignored and went home. Moore missed her, followed her, and found her forlorn and weeping. To compensate for his seeming neglect he wrote for his wife one of his best loved songs, the first verse of which is:

Believe me, if all those endearing young charms,
    Which I gaze on so fondly to-day,
Were to change by tomorrow, and fleet in my arms,
    Like fairy-gifts fading away,
Thou wouldst still be adored, as this moment thou art,
    Let thy loveliness fade as it will,
And around the dear ruin each wish of my heart
    Would entwine itself verdantly still.

On the other hand, Moore wrote a poem whose first verse is:

The time I've lost in wooing,
In watching and pursuing
    The light that lies
    In woman's eyes,
Has been my heart's undoing.
Though Wisdom oft has sought me,
I scorn'd the lore she brought me,
    My only books
    Were woman's looks,
And folly's all they've taught me.

THOMAS MOORE

NORA CREINA

Lesbia hath a beaming eye,
But no one knows for whom it beameth,
    Right and left its arrows fly,
But what they aim at no one dreameth.
    Sweeter 'tis to gaze upon

My Nora's lid that seldom rises;
　　Few its looks, but every one
Like unexpected light surprises!
　　　　O my Nora Creina, dear,
　　My gentle, bashful Nora Creina,
　　　　　Beauty lies
　　　　　In many eyes,
　　But Love in yours, my Nora Creina.

　　Lesbia wears a robe of gold,
But all so close the nymph hath laced it,
　　Not a charm of beauty's mold
Presumes to stay where nature placed it.
　　　　Oh, my Nora's gown for me,
　　That floats as wild as mountain breezes,
　　　　Leaving every beauty free
　　To sink or swell as heaven pleases.
　　　　　Yes, my Nora Creina, dear,
　　My simple, graceful Nora Creina,
　　　　　Nature's dress
　　　　　Is loveliness—
　　The dress *you* wear, my Nora Creina.

　　Lesbia hath a wit refined,
But when its points are gleaming round us,
　　Who can tell if they're designed
To dazzle merely, or to wound us?
　　　　Pillowed on my Nora's heart,
　　In safer slumber Love reposes—
　　　　Bed of peace! whose roughest part
　　Is but the crumpling of the roses.
　　　　　O my Nora Creina, dear,
　　My mild, my artless Nora Creina!
　　　　　Wit, though bright,
　　　　　Hath no such light
　　As warms your eyes, my Nora Creina.

WHAT THE BEE IS TO THE FLOWERET

He.—Nay, if flowers *will* lose their looks,
    When he looks for honeydew,
      Through the leaves that close embower it,
    That, my love, I'll be to you.

She.—What the bank, with verdure glowing,
    Is to waves that wander near,
      Whispering kisses, while they're going,
    That I'll be to you, my dear.

She.—But, they say, the bee's a rover,
    Who will fly when sweets are gone;
    And, when once the kiss is over,
    Faithless brooks will wander on.

He.— Nay, if flowers *will* lose their looks,
    If sunny banks *will* wear away,
      'Tis but right, that bees and brooks
    Should sip and kiss them, while they may.

Lady Dufferin

TERENCE'S FAREWELL.

*Lady Dufferin (1807-1867) was born Helen Selina Sheridan,
granddaughter of Richard Brinsley Sheridan. After the death of
the Earl of Dufferin she married the Earl of Gifford. She wrote
many popular ballads and poems.*

    So, my Kathleen, you're going to leave me
      All alone by myself in this place,
    But I'm sure you will never deceive me—
      Oh no, if there's truth in that face.

Though England's a beautiful city,
  Full of illigant boys—oh, what then?
You would not forget your poor Terence;
  You'll come back to Ould Ireland again.

Och, those English, deceivers by nature,
  Though maybe you'd think them sincere,
They'll say you're a sweet charming creature,
  But don't you believe them, my dear.
No, Kathleen, *agra!* don't be minding
  The flattering speeches they'll make;
Just tell them a poor boy in Ireland
  Is breaking his heart for your sake.

It's folly to keep you from going,
  Though, faith, it's a mighty hard case—
For, Kathleen, you know, there's no knowing
  When next I shall see your sweet face.
And when you come back to me, Kathleen—
  None the better will I be off then—
You'll be spaking such beautiful English,
  Sure, I won't know my Kathleen again.

Eh, now, where's the need of this hurry?
  Don't flutter me so in this way!
I've forgot, 'twixt the grief and the flurry,
  Every word I was maning to say.
Now just wait a minute, I bid ye—
  Can I talk if you bother me so?—
Oh, Kathleen, my blessing go wid ye
  Ev'ry inch of the way that you go.

RICHARD BRINSLEY SHERIDAN

LET THE TOAST PASS

(from *The School for Scandal*)

Richard Brinsley Sheridan (1751-1816) had a career as fantastic as any hero in his plays. His grandfather was a close friend of Dean Swift, his father an actor, his grandchildren English nobility. His marriage involved two duels. He was a member of parliament for thirty years and is buried in Westminster Abbey.

Here's to the maiden of bashful fifteen,
　　Here's to the widow of fifty;
Here's to the flaunting extravagant queen,
　　And here's to the housewife that's thrifty.

Chorus
　　Let the toast pass,
　　Drink to the lass,
I'll warrant she'll prove an excuse for the glass.

Here's to the charmer whose dimples we prize,
　　Now to the maid who has none, sir;
Here's to the girl with a pair of blue eyes,
　　And here's to the nymph with but one, sir!

Here's to the maid with a bosom of snow,
　　And to her that's as brown as a berry;
Here's to the wife, with a face full of woe,
　　And now to the damsel that's merry.

For let 'em be clumsy, or let 'em be slim,
　　Young or ancient, I care not a feather;
So fill the pint bumper quite up to the brim,
　　And let us e'en toast them together:

Chorus
Let the toast pass,

Drink to the lass,
I'll warrant she'll prove an excuse for the glass.

PIERCE FERRITER

HE CHARGES HER TO LAY ASIDE HER WEAPONS

These verses were written in Gaelic by Pierce Ferriter, Chieftan of County Kerry. He was the last of the Catholic Cavaliers to be conquered and hanged by Cromwell. He was noted not only as a warrior but also as a musician and scholar. The translation is by Edward Packenham, 6th Earl of Longford, born in Ireland in 1902 and educated at Eton and Oxford.

I charge you, lady young and fair,
    Straightway to lay your arms aside.
Lay by your armour, would you dare
    To spread the slaughter far and wide?

O lady, lay your armour by,
    Conceal your curling hair also,
For never was a man could fly
    The coils that o'er your bosom flow.

And if you answer, lady fair,
    That north or south you ne'er took life,
Your very eyes, your glance, your air
    Can murder without axe or knife.

And oh! If you but bare your knee,
    If you your soft hand's palm advance,
You'll slaughter many a company.
    What more is done with shield and lance?

Oh, hide your bosom limey white,
    Your naked side conceal from me.

Ah, show them not in all men's sight,
  Your breasts more bright than flowering tree.

And if in you there's shame or fear
  For all the murders you have done,
Let those bright eyes no more appear,
  Those shining teeth be seen of none.

Lady, we tremble far and near!
  Be with these conquests satisfied,
And lest I perish, lady dear,
  Oh, lay those arms of yours aside.

OLIVER ST. JOHN GOGARTY (1878-1957)

TO THE MAIDS NOT TO WALK IN THE WIND

When the wind blows, walk not abroad,
  For, Maids, you may not know
The mad, quaint thoughts which incommode
  Me when the winds do blow.

What though the tresses of the treen
  In doubled beauty move,
With silver added to their green,
  They were not made for Love.

But when your clothes reveal your thighs
  And surge around your knees,
Until from foam you seem to rise,
  As Venus from the seas . . .

Though ye are fair, it is not fair!
  Unless you will be kind,
Till I am dead, and changed to AIR,
  O walk not in the wind!

111

KATHLEEN MAVOURNEEN

Mrs. Julia Crawford (1800-1885), born in County Cavan, collaborated with F. Nichols Crouch, a well-known composer, in the publication of several books of songs.

Kathleen Mavourneen! the gray dawn is breaking,
  The horn of the hunter is heard on the hill;
The lark from her light wing the bright dew is shaking,—
  Kathleen Mavourneen! what slumbering still?
Oh, hast thou forgotten how soon we must sever?
  Oh! hast thou forgotten this day we must part?
It may be for years, and it may be forever!
  Oh, why art thou silent, thou voice of my heart?
Oh! why art thou silent, Kathleen Mavourneen?

Samuel Lover

MOLLY BAWN

Oh! Molly Bawn, why leave me pining,
  All lonely, waiting here for you;
While the stars above are brightly shining
  Because they've nothing else to do?
The flowers late were open keeping,
  To try a rival blush with you;
But their mother, Nature, set them sleeping,
  With their rosy faces washed with dew.

Now the pretty flowers were made to bloom, dear,
  And the pretty stars were made to shine;
And the pretty girls were made for the boys, dear,
  And maybe you were made for mine.

William Butler Yeats

WHEN YOU ARE OLD

Supposedly addressed to Maude Gonne, who married John MacBride, a leader of the Irish Brigade in the Boer War, who was shot by the British after the Easter Week rising in 1916. His son, Sean MacBride, was first Minister of External Affairs of the present Republic of Ireland and is now Secretary General of the International Commission of Jurists in Geneva, Switzerland.

When you are old and gray and full of sleep,
   And nodding by the fire, take down this book,
   And slowly read, and dream of the soft look
Your eyes had once: and of their shadows deep;

How many loved your moments of glad grace,
   And loved your beauty with love false or true,
   But one man loved the pilgrim soul in you,
And loved the sorrows of your changing face.

And bending down beside the glowing bars
   Murmur, a little sadly, how love fled
   And paced upon the mountains overhead
And hid his face amid a crowd of stars.

HUMOR

Few of the best loved Irish poems are funny. Some poems have touches of humor, but even then the general tone of the verses is serious. There were great comedians among the stage Irishmen of America, and there are innumerable jokes at the expense of the Irish, but the poets of Ireland were lyric, serious, or sad.

The Irish are the world's most prolific producers of "Bulls." Sir Boyle Roche, member of the Irish Parliament, is considered the "Father of the Irish Bull." Asked to define a Bull, he said: "Suppose you see three cows standing up in a field, and one of them lying down. That one is the bull."

Two of Sir Boyle's famous Bulls were made in speeches to parliament. In one of them he said: "All along the untrodden pathway of the future I see the footprints of an unseen hand."

Most widely quoted has been his pronouncement: "Why should we beggar ourselves to benefit posterity? What has posterity ever done for us?"

T. P. O'Connor once told the House of Commons, speaking of the Empress of Germany: "Her breadth of mind is masculine in its depth."

BRIAN O'LINN

Brian O'Linn was a gentleman born,
His hair it was long and his beard unshorn,
His teeth were out and his eyes far in—
"I'm a wonderful beauty," says Brian O'Linn!

Brian O'Linn was hard up for a coat,
He borrowed the skin of a neighboring goat,
He buckled the horns right under his chin—
"They'll answer for pistols," says Brian O'Linn!

Brian O'Linn had no breeches to wear,
He got him a sheepskin to make him a pair,
With the fleshy side out and the woolly side in—
"They are pleasant and cool," says Brian O'Linn!

Brian O'Linn had no hat to his head,
He stuck on a pot that was under the shed,
He murdered a cod for the sake of his fin—
" 'T will pass for a feather," says Brian O'Linn!

Brian O'Linn had no shirt to his back,
He went to a neighbor and borrowed a sack,
He puckered a meal-bag under his chin—
"They'll take it for ruffles," said Brian O'Linn!

Brian O'Linn had no shoes at all,
He bought an old pair at a cobbler's stall,
The uppers were broke and the soles were thin—
"They'll do me for dancing," says Brian O'Linn!

Brian O'Linn had no watch for to wear,
He bought a fine turnip and scooped it out fair,
He slipped a live cricket right under the skin—
"They'll think it is ticking," says Brian O'Linn!

115

Brian O'Linn and his wife and wife's mother,
They all crossed over the bridge together,
The bridge broke down and they all tumbled in—
"We'll go home by water," says Brian O'Linn!

ANONYMOUS

COCKLES AND MUSSELS

In Dublin's fair city,
Where the girls are so pretty,
   I first set my eyes on sweet Mollie Malone.
She wheeled her wheel-barrow
Through streets broad and narrow,
   Crying, "Cockles and mussels, alive, alive, oh!

         "Alive, alive, oh!
         Alive, alive, oh!"
   Crying, "Cockles and mussels, alive, alive, oh!"

She was a fishmonger,
But sure 'twas no wonder,
   For so were her father and mother before.
And they both wheeled their barrow
Through streets broad and narrow,
   Crying, "Cockles and mussels, alive, alive, oh!

         "Alive, alive, oh! &c."

She died of a fever,
And none could relieve her,
   And that was the end of sweet Mollie Malone.
But her ghost wheels her barrow
Through streets broad and narrow,
   Crying, "Cockles and mussels, alive, alive, oh!"

         "Alive, alive, oh! &c."

Epitaph on a gravestone in a churchyard in Kilmurry, County Clare:

> This stone was raised by Sarah's lord,
> Not Sarah's virtues to record—
> For they're well known to all the town,
> But it was raised to keep her down.

OLIVER GOLDSMITH (1728-1774)

AN ELEGY ON THE GLORY OF HER SEX, MRS. MARY BLAIZE

Good people all, with one accord,
  Lament for Madam Blaize,
Who never wanted a good word—
  From those who spoke her praise.

The needy seldom passed her door,
  And always found her kind;
She freely lent to all the poor—
  Who left a pledge behind.

She strove the neighborhood to please,
  With manners wondrous winning;
And never followed wicked ways—
  Unless when she was sinning.

At church, in silks and satins new,
  With hoop of monstrous size,
She never slumbered in her pew—
  But when she shut her eyes.

Her love was sought, I do aver,
  By twenty beaux and more;
The king himself has followed her—
  When she has walked before.

117

But now her wealth and finery fled,
   Her hangers-on cut short all;
The doctors found, when she was dead—
   Her last disorder mortal.

Let us lament, in sorrow sore,
   For Kent-street well may say,
That had she lived a twelvemonth more—
   She had not died today.

ANONYMOUS

GARRYOWEN

Let Bacchus' sons be not dismayed,
But join with me each jovial blade
Come booze and sing, and lend your aid
   To help me with the chorus;

   Instead of Spa we'll drink brown ale,
   And pay the reckoning on the nail;
   No man for debt shall go to gaol
      From Garryowen in glory!

We are the boys that take delight in
Smashing the Limerick lights when lighting,
Through the streets like sporters fighting,
   And tearing all before us.

We'll break windows, we'll break doors.
The watch knock down by threes and fours;
Then let the doctors work their cures,
   And tinker up our bruises.

We'll beat the bailiffs, out of fun,
We'll make the mayor and sheriffs run;

We are the boys no man dares dun,
  If he regards a whole skin.

Our hearts so stout, have got us fame,
For soon 'tis known from whence we came:
Where'er we go they dread the name
Of Garryowen in glory.

Johnny Cornell's tall and straight,
And in his limbs he is complate;
He'll pitch a bar of any weight,
  From Garryowen to Thomond Gate.

Garryowen is gone to wrack
Since Johnny Connell went to Cork,
Though Darby O'Brien leapt over the dock
  In spite of all the soldiers.

ANONYMOUS

THE RAKES OF MALLOW

Beauing, belle-ing, dancing, drinking,
Breaking windows, damning, sinking,
Ever raking, never thinking,
  Live the rakes of Mallow.

Spending faster than it comes,
Beating waiters, bailiffs, duns,
Bacchus's true-begotten sons,
  Live the rakes of Mallow.

One time nought but claret drinking,
Then like politicians thinking

To raise the sinking funds when sinking,
    Live the rakes of Mallow.

When at home with dadda dying,
Still for Mallow water crying;
But where there's good claret plying,
    Live the rakes of Mallow.

Living short but merry lives;
Going where the devil drives;
Having sweethearts, but no wives,
    Live the rakes of Mallow.

Racking tenants, stewards teasing,
Swiftly spending, slowly raising,
Wishing to spend all their days in
    Raking as at Mallow.

Then to end this raking life
They get sober, take a wife,
Ever after live in strife,
    And wish again for Mallow.

ANONYMOUS

MOLLY BRANNIGAN

An old street ballad popularized by John McCormack.

Mam, dear, did ye never hear of pretty Molly Brannigan?
Troth, an' she's left me, and I'll never be a man again,
Not a spot on me hide will the summer's sun e'er tan
        again
Since Molly's gone and left me here—alone for to die.

The spot where me heart was ye'd aisy rowl a turnip in.

'Tis as large as any pavin' stone from Dublin to the
    Divil's Glin.
If she wished to take another, sure, she might have left
    mine back again,
Or not have gone and left me here alone for to die.

Mam, dear, I remember whin the milkin' time was past
    and gone
We walked through the meadows, and she swore I was
    the only one
That ever she could love—and now, the false and cruel
    one—
For all that she's gone—and left me here for to die.

Mam, dear, I remember whin comin' home the rain
    began.
I wrapped me freize coat round her—and ne'er the
    waistcoat had I on.
Me shirt was rather fine drawn—but, Oh, the false and
    cruel one—
For all that she's gone and left me here for to die.

The left side of me carcass is as wake as wather gruel,
    Mam.
There's not a pick upon me bones since Molly proved
    so cruel, Mam.
Oh, if I had a blundergun I'd go and fight a duel, Mam,
For, sure, I'd better shoot meself than live here to die.

I'm cool and detarmined as a live salamander, Mam,
Will ye come to me wake whin I go the long meander,
    Mam?
I'll think meself as valiant as the famous Alexander,
    Mam,
Whin I hear ye cryin' o'er me "Arrah, why did ye die?"

WHEN YEATS SHAKES HANDS

When Yeats shakes hands you feel that he
Is just as sweet as he can be—
The very pink of courtesy.

He doesn't mind how much you stare;
Say what you will, he doesn't care.
You see, he doesn't know you're there.

His gaze is fixed far, far away,
On some deep glade where fairies play
In robes of green and silver-gray.

And while the horns of Elfland toot
He doesn't care a Celtic hoot
If you are vocal or are mute.

He's looking past your starboard ear,
And has no notion you are near.
Of course you feel a little queer.

But think not you are coldly sped:
'Tis as the Dublin copper said:
" 'Tis but the po'thry in his head."

INVECTIVE

The Irish have a gift for invective. Two frequently quoted poems of rebellion are notable chiefly for their opening curses. The tribute of Thomas Osborn Davis to Owen Roe O'Neill begins:

> "Did they dare, did they dare, to slay Eoghan Ruadh
> O'Neill?"
> "Yes, they slew with poison him they feared to meet
> with steel!"
> "May God wither up their hearts! May their blood cease
> to flow!
> May they walk in living death, who poisoned Eoghan
> Ruadh!"

The words John Savage placed in the mouth of the clansman who sees the head of his chief, Shaun O'Neill, on a pole before Dublin Castle gate, are so blasphemous that they were always omitted from Irish schoolbooks carrying the remainder of the poem.

> "God's wrath upon the Saxon; may they never know the
> pride
> Of dying on the battle-field, their broken spear beside;

123

May every light from cross of Christ that saves the heart
    of man
Be hid in clouds of blood before it reach the Saxon clan;
For sure, O God, and You know all, whose thought for
    all sufficed,
To expiate these Saxons sins, they'd want another Christ."

When a reviewer in a Dublin paper was critical of The Play-
boy of the Western World, the author replied as follows:

Lord confound this surly sister,
Blight her brow with blotch and blister,
Cramp her larynx, lungs and liver,
In her guts a galling give her.

Let her live to earn her dinners
In Mountjoy with seedy sinners:
Lord, this judgment quickly bring,
And I'm your servant, J. M. Synge.

JEREMIAH JOSEPH CALLAHAN

Translated from the Gaelic

THE LAMENT FOR O'SULLIVAN BEARE

(Made by His Nurse)

Jeremiah Joseph Callahan (1795-1829) entered Trinity College
to study medicine but won prizes in poetry. He worked as a
teacher, traveled through Ireland collecting Gaelic songs and
stories and converting them into English verse. The body of
O'Sullivan Beare is said to have been dragged behind a boat
from Bearhaven to Cork where the head was cut off and put on
a spike above the jail. The words are those of his aged nurse.

The sun of Ivera
No longer shines brightly,
The voice of her music
No longer is sprightly;
No more to her maidens
The light dance is dear,
Since the death of our darling
O'Sullivan Beare.

Scully! thou false one
You basely betrayed him;
In his strong hour of need
When thy right hand should aid him;
He fed thee—he clad thee—
You had all could delight thee:
You left him, you sold him
May heaven requite thee!

Scully! May all kinds
Of evil attend thee!
On thy dark road of life
May no kind one befriend thee!
May fevers long burn thee,
And agues long freeze thee!
May the strong hand of God
In his red anger seize thee!

Had he died calmly
I would not deplore him;
Or if the wild strife
Of the sea-war closed o'er him:
But with ropes round his white limbs
Through Ocean to trail him,
Like a fish after slaughter
'Tis therefore I wail him.

Long may the curse
Of his people pursue them;

Scully that sold him
And soldier that slew him!
One glimpse of Heaven's light
May they see never!
May the hearthstone of Hell
Be their best bed forever!

In the hole where the vile hands
Of soldiers had laid thee,
Unhonored, unshrouded,
And headless they laid thee,
No eye to rain o'er thee,
No dirge to lament thee,
No friend to deplore thee!

Dear head of my darling
How gory and pale
These aged eyes see thee,
High spiked on their jail!
That cheek in the summer sun
Ne'er shall grow warm;
Nor that eye e'er catch light
From the flash of the storm!

A curse, blessed ocean,
Is on thy green water
From the Haven of Cork
To Ivera of slaughter:
Since the billows were dyed
With the red wounds of fear
Of Muirtach Og
Our O'Sullivan Beare!

DOUGLAS HYDE

Translated from the Gaelic

BRUADAR AND SMITH AND GLINN

Douglas Hyde, son of a Protestant rector, made a vast contribution to Irish literature and became President of the Irish Free State from 1938 to 1944. When, as a divinity student, he entered Trinity College, he was asked what languages he knew. He replied: "English, German, French, Latin, Greek, and Hebrew, but I dream in Irish." From 1893 to 1915 he was leader of the Gaelic League.

Bruadar and Smith and Glinn,
　Amen, dear God, I pray,
May they lie low in waves of woe,
　And tortures slow each day!
　　Amen!

Bruadar and Smith and Glinn
　May flails of sorrow flay!
Cause for lamenting, snares and cares
　Be theirs by night and day!
　　Amen!

Blindness come down on Smith,
　Palsy on Bruadar come,
Amen, O King of Brightness! Smite
　Glinn in his members numb,
　　Amen!

Smith in the pangs of pain,
　Stumbling on Bruadar's path,
King of the Elements, Oh, Amen!
　Let loose on Glinn Thy Wrath.
　　Amen!

For Bruadar gape the grave,
  Up-shovel for Smith the mould,
Amen, O King of the Sunday! Leave
  Glinn in the devil's hold.
          Amen!

Terrors on Bruadar rain,
  And pain upon pain on Glinn,
Amen, O King of the Stars! And Smith
  May the devil be linking him.
          Amen!

Glinn in a shaking ague,
  Cancer on Bruadar's tongue,
Amen, O King of the Heavens! and Smith
  Forever stricken dumb.
          Amen!

Thirst but no drink for Glinn,
  Smith in a cloud of grief,
Amen! O King of the Saints; and rout
  Bruadar without relief.
          Amen!

Smith without child or heir,
  And Bruadar bare of store,
Amen, O King of the Friday! Tear
  For Glinn his black heart's core.
          Amen!

Bruadar with nerveless limbs,
  Hemp strangling Glinn's last breath,
Amen, O King of the World's Light!
  And Smith in grips with death.
          Amen!

Glinn stiffening for the tomb,

Smith wasting to decay,
Amen, O King of the Thunder's gloom,
And Bruadar sick alway.
　　　Amen!

Smith like a sieve of holes,
　Bruadar with throat decay,
Amen, O King of the Orders! Glinn
　A buck-show every day.
　　　Amen!

Hell-hounds to hunt for Smith,
　Glinn led to hang on high,
Amen, O King of the Judgment Day!
And Bruadar rotting by.
　　　Amen!

Showers of want and blame,
　Reproach, and shame of face,
Smite them all three, and smite again,
　Amen, O King of Grace!
　　　Amen!

Melt, may the three, away,
　Bruadar and Smith and Glinn,
Fall in a swift and sure decay
　And lose, but never win.
　　　Amen!

May pangs pass through thee, Smith
　(Let the wind not take my prayer),
May I see before the year is out
　Thy heart's blood flowing there.
　　　Amen!

Leave Smith no place nor land,
　Let Bruadar wander wide,

May the Devil stand at Glinn's right hand,
  And Glinn to him be tied.
      Amen!

I accuse both Glinn and Bruadar,
  And Smith I accuse to God,
May a breach and a gap be upon the three,
  And the Lord's avenging rod.
      Amen!

Each one of the wicked three
  Who raised against me their hand,
May fire from heaven come down and slay
  This day their perjured band,
      Amen!

May none of their race survive,
  May God destroy them all,
Each curse of the psalms in the holy books
  Of the prophets upon them fall.
      Amen!

Blight skull, and ear, and skin,
  And hearing, and voice, and sight,
Amen! before the year be out,
  Blight, Son of the Virgin, blight.
      Amen!

May my curses hot and red
  And all I have said this day,
Strike the Black Peeler, too,
  Amen, dear God, I pray!
      Amen!

NELL FLAHERTY'S DRAKE

My name it is Nell, right candid I tell,
  And I live near a dell I ne'er will deny,
I had a large drake, the truth for to spake,
  My grandfather left me when going to die;
He was merry and sound, and would weigh twenty
      pound,
  The universe round would I rove for his sake.
Bad luck to the robber, be he drunken or sober,
  That murdered Nell Flaherty's beautiful drake.

His neck it was green, and rare to be seen,
  He was fit for a queen of the highest degree.
His body so white, it would you delight,
  He was fat, plump, and heavy, and brisk as a bee.
This dear little fellow, his legs they were yellow,
  He could fly like a swallow, or swim like a hake,
But some wicked habbage, to grease his white cabbage,
  Has murdered Nell Flaherty's beautiful drake!

May his pig never grunt, may his cat never hunt,
  That a ghost may him haunt in the dark of the night.
May his hens never lay, may his horse never neigh,
  May his goat fly away like an old paper kite;
May his duck never quack, may his goose be turned black
  And pull down his stack with her long yellow beak.
May the scurvy and itch never part from the britch
  Of the wretch that murdered Nell Flaherty's drake!

May his rooster ne'er crow, may his bellows not blow,
  Nor potatoes to grow—may he never have none—
May his cradle not rock, may his chest have no lock,
  May his wife have no frock for to shade her backbone.
That the bugs and the fleas may this wicked wretch tease,

And a piercing north breeze make him tremble and
    shake.
May a four-years'-old bug build a nest in the lug
    Of the monster that murdered Nell Flaherty's drake.

May his pipe never smoke, may his tea-pot be broke,
    And to add to the joke may his kettle not boil;
May he be poorly fed till the hour he is dead.
    May he always be fed on lobscouse and fish oil.
May he swell with the gout till his grinders fall out,
    May he roar, howl, and shout with a horrid toothache,
May his temple wear horns and his toes carry corns,
    The wretch that murdered Nell Flaherty's drake.

May his dog yelp and howl with both hunger and cold,
    May his wife always scold till his brains go astray.
May the curse of each hag, that ever carried a bag,
    Light down on the wag till his head it turns gray.
May monkeys still bite him, and mad dogs affright him,
    And every one slight him, asleep or awake.
May wasps ever gnaw him, and jackdaws ever claw him,
    The monster that murdered Nell Flaherty's drake.

But the only good news I have to diffuse,
    Is of Peter Hughes and Paddy McCade,
And crooked Ned Manson, and big-nosed Bob Hanson,
    Each one had a grandson of my beautiful drake.
Oh! my bird he has dozens of nephews and cousins,
    And one I must have, or my heart it will break.
To keep my mind easy, or else I'll run crazy,
    And so ends the song of my beautiful drake.

PATRICK O'KELLY

THE CURSE OF DONERAILE

When Patrick O'Kelly lost his watch in Doneraile, he wrote some verses which quickly became popular. Lady Doneraile then replaced the lost "watch and seal," and O'Kelly wrote another poem, "Blessings on Doneraile." The first verses have always been more popular.

Alas! how dismal is my tale,
I lost my watch in Doneraile.
My Dublin watch, my chain and seal,
Pilfered at once in Doneraile.
May Fire and Brimstone never fail,
To fall in showers on Doneraile.
May all the leading fiends assail,
The thieving town of Doneraile,
As lightnings flash across the vale,
So down to Hell with Doneraile.
The fate of Pompey at Pharsale,
Be that the curse of Doneraile.
May Beef, or Mutton, Lamb or Veal
Be never found in Doneraile.
But Garlic Soup and scurvy Kale,
Be still the food for Doneraile.
And forward as the creeping snail,
Th' industry be, of Doneraile.
May Heaven a chosen curse entail,
On rigid, rotten Doneraile.
May Sun and Moon forever fail,
To beam their lights on Doneraile.
May every pestilential gale,
Blast that cursed spot called Doneraile.
May not a Cuckoo, Thrush, or Quail,
Be ever heard in Doneraile.
May Patriots, Kings and Commonweal,
Despise and harass Doneraile.

May ev'ry Post, Gazette, and Mail,
Sad tidings bring of Doneraile.
May loudest thunders ring a peal,
To blind and deafen Doneraile.
May vengeance fall at head and tail,
From North to South at Doneraile.
May profit light and tardy sale,
Still damp the trade of Doneraile.
May Fame resound a dismal tale,
Whene'er she lights on Doneraile.
May Egypt's plagues at once prevail,
To thin the knaves of Doneraile.
May frost and snow, and sleet and hail
Benumb each joint in Doneraile.
May wolves and bloodhounds trace and trail,
The cursèd crew of Doneraile.
May Oscar with his fiery flail,
To Atoms thrash all Doneraile.
May every mischief fresh and stale,
Abide henceforth in Doneraile.
May all from Belfast to Kinsale,
Scoff, curse, and damn you, Doneraile.
May neither Flow'r nor Oatenmeal,
Be found or known in Doneraile.
May want and woe each joy curtail,
That e'er was known in Doneraile.
May no one coffin want a nail,
That wraps a rogue in Doneraile.
May all the thieves that rob and steal,
The gallows meet in Doneraile.
May all the sons of Granuale,
Blush at the thieves of Doneraile.
May mischief big as Norway whale,
O'erwhelm the knaves of Doneraile.
May curses wholesale and retail,
Pour with full force on Doneraile.
May ev'ry transport wont to sail,
A convict bring from Doneraile.

May ev'ry churn and milking pail,
Fall dry to staves in Doneraile.
May cold and hunger still congeal,
The stagnant blood of Doneraile.
May ev'ry hour new woes reveal,
That Hell reserves for Doneraile.
May ev'ry chosen ill prevail,
O'er all the Imps of Doneraile.
May no one wish or prayer avail,
To soothe the woes of Doneraile.
May th' Inquisition straight impale,
The rapparees of Doneraile.
May curse of Sodom now prevail,
And sink to ashes Doneraile.
May Charon's Boat triumphant sail,
Completely manned from Doneraile.
Oh! may my Couplets never fail,
To find new curse for Doneraile.
And may Grim Pluto's inner jail,
For ever groan with Doneraile.

Patrick O'Kelly had a good opinion of his poetic talents. He wrote:

> *'T would take a Byron and a Scott, I tell ye*
> *Combined in one to make a Pat O'Kelly.*

His apologies to Doneraile follow:

BLESSINGS ON DONERAILE

How vastly pleasing is my tale
I found my watch in Doneraile.
My Dublin watch, my chain and seal
Were all restored at Doneraile.
May fire and brimstone ever fail
To hurt or injure Doneraile.
May neither friend nor foe assail
The splendid town of Doneraile.
May lightning never singe the vale
That leads to generous Doneraile.
May Pompey's fate and old Pharsale
Be still reversed at Doneraile.
May beef and mutton, lamb and veal
Plentyful be in Doneraile.
May garlic soup and scurvy kale
No palate spoil in Doneraile.
May neither frog nor creeping snail
Subtract the crops of Doneraile.
May Heaven each chosen bliss entail
On honest, friendly Doneraile.
May Sol and Luna never fail
O'erflow with cream at Doneraile.
May cold and hunger ne'er congeal
The good rich blood of Doneraile.
May every day new joys reveal
To crown the bliss of Doneraile.
May every soft ambrosial gale
Sweet odours waft to Doneraile.
May no corroding ill prevail
To damp the joys of Doneraile.
May the Inquisition ne'er impale
Or hurt a limb from Doneraile.
May Sodom's curse forever fail

To hurt and injure Doneraile.
But may each wish and prayer prevail
To crown with peace sweet Doneraile.

JAMES STEPHENS

RIGHTEOUS ANGER

James Stephens is known for his Crock of Gold *and his* Irish Fairy Tales, *as well as for several books of poetry.*

The lanky hank of a she in the inn over there
Nearly killed me for asking the loan of a glass of beer:
May the devil grip the whey-faced slut by the hair,
And beat bad manners out of her skin for a year.

That parboiled imp, with the hardest jaw you will see
On virtue's path, and a voice that would rasp the dead,
Came roaring and raging the minute she looked on me,
And threw me out of the house on the back of my head!

If I asked her master he'd give me a cask a day;
But she, with the beer at hand, not a gill would arrange!
May she marry a ghost and bear him a kitten, and may
The High King of Glory permit her to get the mange.

JAMES H. COUSINS

A CURSE ON A CLOSED GATE

*James H. Cousins (1873-1955), born in Belfast, helped organ-
ize the Irish National Theater, published several books, and then
became Professor of English in a university in India.*

Be this the fate
Of the man who would shut his gate
On the stranger, gentle or simple, early or late.

When his mouth with a day's long hunger and thirst
      would wish
For the savour of salted fish,
Let him sit and eat his fill of an empty dish.

To the man of that ilk,
Let water stand in his churn, instead of milk
That turns a calf's coat silk.

And under the gloomy night
May never a thatch made tight
Shut out the clouds from his sight.

Above the ground or below it,
Good cheer, may he never know it,
Nor a tale by the fire, nor a dance on the road, nor a song
      by a wandering poet.

Till he open his gate
To the stranger, early or late,
And turn back the stone of his fate.

EMIGRATION

There have been five main stages of Irish emigration:

1. Following barbarian conquests of Christian Europe, saints and scholars from unconquered Ireland founded schools and monasteries through the sixth, seventh, and eighth centuries, helping to restore Christianity and civilization.

2. When Cromwell conquered Ireland, he turned more than two-thirds of the land over to English adventurers and caused the transportation of many thousands of young men and women and children to America to serve the colonists. In addition to Cromwell's slave laborers, many Catholic gentry migrated—particularly to Maryland.

3. When William of Orange defeated the forces of James II at Limerick, he permitted Patrick Sarsfield to take his Irish regiments to France to form the Irish Brigade. During the next century France, Spain, Austria, and even Russia recruited hundreds of thousands of soldiers from Ireland. England seems to have done little to prevent the departure of potential rebels.

4. Emigrants from Ireland to America in the 1700's were largely Presbyterians from Ulster, resentful of their landlords, of the Established Church, and of the laws by which England had suc-

cessively ruined their woolen industry, their linen trade, their hemp and cotton manufactures, and their tobacco growing.

5. In the 1840's came the potato famine which, by starvation, "the fever," and emigration, reduced the population of Ireland from nine million to five million.

French ships smuggled wines, brandies, silks, etc. to harbors in Kerry, Galway, Clare, Cork, and Limerick. Return cargoes were often whole companies—known as "Wild Geese"—recruited for foreign service. At one time there were thirty Irish generals in the Austrian Army. Spain had three Irish regiments. Last colonel of the Irish Brigade, in 1792, was Count O'Connell, uncle of Daniel O'Connell, "The Liberator."

Ambrose O'Higgins, son of a Mayo farmer, became a Spanish major general, Count of Balenar, Marquis of Osorno, Captain General of Chili, and Viceroy of Peru. His son, Bernard, is one of the great heroes of South America, corresponding, in a way, to George Washington in North America.

The Irish Brigade is memorialized in the three following poems by Thomas Osborn Davis.

Thomas Osborn Davis

THE BATTLE EVE OF THE BRIGADE

The mess-tent is full, and the glasses are set,
And the gallant Count Thomond is president yet;
The vet'ran arose, like an uplifted lance,
Crying—"Comrades, a health to the monarch of France!"
With bumpers and cheers they have done as he bade,
For King Louis is loved by The Irish Brigade.

"A health to King James," and they bent as they quaffed;
"Here's to George the *Elector*," and fiercely they laughed;

"Good luck to the girls we wooed long ago,
Where Shannon, and Barrow, and Blackwater flow;"
"God prosper Old Ireland,"—you'd think them afraid,
So pale grew the chiefs of The Irish Brigade.

"But, surely, that light cannot come from our lamp?
And the noise—are they *all* getting drunk in the camp?"
"Hurrah! boys, the morning of battle is come,
And the *generale's* beating on many a drum."
So they rush from the revel to join the parade;
For the van is the right of The Irish Brigade.

They fought as they revelled, fast, fiery, and true,
And, though victors, they left on the field not a few;
And they, who survived, fought and drank as of yore,
But the land of their heart's hope they never saw more;
For in far foreign fields, from Dunkirk to Belgrade,
Lie the soldiers and chiefs of The Irish Brigade.

THOMAS OSBORN DAVIS

THE BATTLE OF FONTENOY

The Irish Brigade won the battle but lost one-fourth of its officers and one-third of its men. George II said: "Cursed be the laws that deprive me of such subjects."

Thrice, at the huts of Fontenoy, the English column
    failed,
And, twice, the lines of Saint Antoine, the Dutch in
    vain assailed;
For town and slope were filled with fort and flanking
    battery,
And well they swept the English ranks, and Dutch
    auxiliary.

As vainly through De Berri's wood, the British soldiers
    burst,
The French artillery drove them back, diminished, and
    dispersed,
The bloody Duke of Cumberland beheld with anxious
    eye,
And ordered up his last reserve, his latest chance to try.
On Fontenoy—on Fontenoy, how fast his generals ride!
And mustering come his chosen troops, like clouds at
    even-tide.

Six thousand English veterans in stately column tread,
Their cannon blaze in front and flank, Lord Hay is at
    their head;
Steady they step adown the slope—steady they climb
    the hill;
Steady they load—steady they fire, moving right onward
    still,
Betwixt the wood and Fontenoy, as though a furnace
    blast,
Through rampart, trench, and palisade, and bullets
    showering fast;
And on the open plain above they 'rose and kept their
    course,
With ready fire and grim resolve, that mocked at hostile
    force:
Past Fontenoy—past Fontenoy, while thinner grow their
    ranks—
They break, as broke the Zuyder Zee through Holland's
    ocean banks.

More idly than the summer flies, French tirailleurs rush
    'round:
As stubble to the lava tide, French squadrons strew the
    ground;
Bomb-shell and grape, and round-shot tore, still on they
    marched and fired—

Fast, from each volley, grenadier and voltigeur retired.
"Push on, my household cavalry!" King Louis madly
    cried;
To death they rush, but rude their shock—not un-
    avenged they died.
On through the camp the column trod—King Louis
    turns his rein:
"Not yet, my liege," Saxe interposed, "the Irish troops
    remain!"
And Fontenoy, famed Fontenoy, had been a Waterloo,
Were not these exiles ready then, fresh, vehement, and
    true.

"Lord Clare," he says, "you have your wish, there are
    your Saxon foes!"
The marshal almost smiled to see, so furiously he goes!
How fierce the look these exiles wear, who're wont to be
    so gay,
The treasured wrongs of fifty years are in their hearts
    to-day—
The treaty broken, ere the ink wherewith 'twas writ,
    could dry,
Their plundered homes, their ruined shrines, their
    women's parting cry—
Their priesthood hunted down like wolves, their
    country overthrown,
Each looks, as if revenge for all were staked on him
    alone.
On Fontenoy, on Fontenoy, nor ever yet elsewhere,
Rushed on to fight a nobler band than these proud
    exiles were.

O'Brien's voice is hoarse with joy, as, halting, he
    commands,
"Fix bay'nets"—"charge,"—like mountain storm, rush
    on these fiery bands!
Thin is the English column now, and faint their volleys
    grow,

Yet, must'ring all the strength they have, they make a
    gallant show.
They dress their ranks upon the hill to face that battle
    wind—
Their bayonets the breakers' foam; like rocks, the men
    behind!
One volley crashes from their line, when, through the
    surging smoke,
With empty guns clutched in their hands, the headlong
    Irish broke.
On Fontenoy, on Fontenoy, hark to that fierce huzza!
"Revenge! remember Limerick! dash down the
    Sassenagh!"

Like lions leaping at a fold, when mad with hunger's
    pang,
Right up against the English line the Irish exiles sprang;
Bright was their steel, 'tis bloody now, their guns are
    filled with gore;
Through shattered ranks, and severed files, and trampled
    flags they tore;
The English strove with desperate strength, paused,
    rallied, staggered, fled—
The green hill-side is matted close with dying and with
    dead;
Across the plain, and far away passed on that hideous
    wrack,
While cavalier and fantassin dash in upon their track.
On Fontenoy—on Fontenoy, like eagles in the sun,
With bloody plumes the Irish stand—the field is fought
    and won!

THOMAS OSBORN DAVIS

THE GIRL I LEFT BEHIND ME

The dames of France are fond and free,
  And Flemish lips are willing,
And soft the maids of Italy,
  And Spanish eyes are thrilling;
Still, though I bask beneath their smile,
  Their charms fail to bind me,
And my heart flies back to Erin's isle,
  To the girl I left behind me.

For she's as fair as Shannon's side,
  And purer than its water,
But she refused to be my bride
  Though many a year I sought her;
Yet, since to France I sailed away,
  Her letters oft remind me
That I promised never to gainsay
  The girl I left behind me.

She says—"My own dear love, come home,
  My friends are rich and many,
Or else abroad with you I'll roam
  A soldier stout as any;
If you'll not come, nor let me go,
  I'll think you have resigned me."
My heart nigh broke when I answered—No!
  To the girl I left behind me.

For never shall my true love brave
  A life of war and toiling;
And never as a skulking slave
  I'll tread my native soil on;
But, were it free, or to be freed,
  The battle's close would find me
To Ireland bound—nor message need
  From the girl I left behind me.

145

Of the signers of the Declaration of Independence, Thornton, Wilson, Taylor, and Smith were natives of Ireland; McKean, Read, and Rutledge were of Irish parentage; Lynch and Carroll were grandsons of Irishmen; and Whipple and Hancock had Irish mothers.

The First Continental Congress in July, 1775, adopted an "Address to the People of Ireland" which said:

You had ever been friendly to the rights of mankind; and we acknowledge with pleasure and gratitude that your nation has produced patriots who have nobly distinguished themselves in the cause of humanity and America.

In 1779 a committee of the British House of Commons heard testimony that half the soldiers in Washington's armies were born in Ireland. On the rolls of these Colonial armies were 872 Kellys. They outnumbered all other names—even the Smiths. There were 230 O'Briens. Many of the Anglican colonists were reluctant to take up arms against a king who was also head of their church. The Presbyterian and Catholic Irish had no such scruples.

The father of Daniel Boone was an Irish Catholic. Two other Irishmen preceded him in exploring Kentucky: John Finley and James McBride. George Rogers Clark was also Irish. Sam Houston, first President of Texas, was of Irish parentage. Abraham Lincoln and Thomas Jefferson both had Irish ancestors. George Washington was a member of The Friendly Sons of St. Patrick.

Among the soldiers of fortune who dropped their commissions in Europe to join the American rebellion against England were: Commandant O'Donnell, who had been a colonel in the Polish army; Robert McCarthy Moore, a captain in the French army; and Baron O'Cahill, a colonel in the Bavarian army. Eleven of Washington's generals were of Irish lineage. John Barry was the first commodore of the United States Navy.

WILLIAM B. McBURNEY (1844-1890)

THE GOOD SHIP CASTLE DOWN

(A rebel chaunt—A.D. 1776)

Oh, how she plowed the ocean, the good ship *Castle Down*,
That day we hung our colors out, the Harp without the Crown!
A gallant barque, she topped the wave, and fearless hearts were we,
With guns and pikes and bayonets, a stalwart company.
'Twas sixteen years from Thurot; and sweeping down the bay
The "Siege of Carrickfergus" so merrily we did play:
By the old castle's foot we went with three right hearty cheers,
And waved aloft our green cockades, for we were Volunteers.
Volunteers!
Oh, we were in our prime that day, stout Irish Volunteers.

'Twas when we heaved our anchor on the breast of smooth Garmoyle
Our guns spoke out in thunder: "Adieu, sweet Irish soil!"
At Whiteabbey and Greencastle, and Hollywood so gay,
Were hundreds waving handkerchiefs and many a loud huzza.
Our voices o'er the water struck the hollow mountains round—
Young Freedom, struggling at her birth, might utter such a sound.
By that green slope beside Belfast we cheer'd and cheer'd it still—
For they had changed its name that year, and they called it Bunker's Hill—

Bunker's Hill!
Oh, were our hands but with our hearts in the trench at
        Bunker's Hill!

Our ship cleared out for Quebec; but thither little bent,
Up some New England river, to run her keel we meant;
So we took a course due north as round old Black Head
        we steered,
Till Ireland bore southwest by south, and Fingal's rock
        appeared.
Then on the poop stood Webster, while the ship hung
        flutterlingly,
About to take her tack across the wide, wide ocean sea—
He pointed to th' Atlantic, "Sure, yon's no place for
        slaves;
Haul down these British badges, for Freedom rules the
        waves—
Rules the waves!"
Three hundred strong men answered, shouting "Freedom
        rules the waves!"

Then all together rose and hauled the British ensign
        down,
And up we hauled our Irish green, without the British
        Crown.
Emblazoned there a Golden Harp like a maiden
        undefiled,
A shamrock wreath around her head, looked o'er the
        sea and smiled.
A hundred days with adverse wind we kept our course
        afar,
On the hundredth day came bearing down a British
        sloop of war,
When they spied our flag they fired a gun, but as they
        neared us fast,
Old Andrew Jackson went aloft and nailed it to the
        mast—
To the mast!
A soldier was old Jackson, and he made our colors fast.

Patrick Henry was our captain, as brave as ever sailed.
"Now we must do or die" said he, "for the Green Flag"
is nailed.
Silently came the sloop along; and silently we lay
Flat, till with cheers and loud broadside the fore began
the fray.
Then boarders o'er the bulwarks, like shuttlecocks we
cast;
One close discharge from all our guns cut down the
tapering mast.
"Now British tars! St. George's Cross is trailing in the
sea—
How d'ye like the greeting and the handsel of the Free?—
Of the Free!
How like you, lads, the greeting of the men who will
be free?"

They answered us with cannon, as befitted well their
fame;
And to shoot away our Irish flag each gunner took his
aim;
They ripped it up in ribbons till it fluttered in the air,
And riddled it with shot-holes till no Golden Harp was
there;
But through the ragged holes the sky did glance and
gleam in light,
Just as the twinkling stars shine through God's unfurled
flag at night.
With dropping fire we sang, "Good-night, and fare ye
well, brave tars!"
Our captain looked aloft: "By heaven! the flag is Stripes
and Stars!"
Stripes and Stars!
So into Boston port we sailed beneath the Stripes and
Stars.

In the eighteenth century Irish peasants lived on potatoes and water. If they had a cow, butter could be made and sold, and the family enjoyed buttermilk and skim-milk with their potatoes. Wages were from five to ten pence a day. Arthur Young reported as follows on the general living expenses for a gentleman in Limerick:

> I was told of a person's keeping a carriage, four horses, three men, three maids, good table, a wife, three children, and a nurse, and all for 500 pounds a year.

The great mass of Irish people were on a bare subsistence diet when the great famine of the 1840's struck. True, they raised cattle and sheep and pigs, but those went to the landlord for rents which were raised as fast as production increased. The famine led to epidemics of disease and led all who could find boat fares to emigrate. Many committed crimes and gladly confessed them in order to be sentenced to transportation.

One of the most bitter critics of the British government and of the Irish landlords was Lady Wilde (1820-1896), mother of Oscar Wilde. This Irish patriot was the daughter of a Protestant clergyman and the wife of a distinguished Dublin physician. While still in her teens she began secretly contributing to a rebel publication, The Nation, under the name "Speranza." For years her identity was not known even to the editor of the magazine. When an editor was on trial for his life in "Forty-Eight," Lady Wilde astounded all present by arising among the spectators and informing the judges that she had written the article which had just been offered as proof of the defendant's treason. Later she published several volumes of prose, including The Ancient Legends of Ireland, Irish in America, and translations from the French and German. Her best known verses were about the Irish famine.

Lady Wilde (Speranza)

THE FAMINE YEAR

Weary men, what reap ye?—"Golden corn for the
    stranger."
What sow ye?—"Human corses that wait for the
    avenger."
Fainting forms, hunger-stricken, what see ye in the offing?
"Stately ships to bear our food away amid the stranger's
    scoffing."
There's a proud array of soldiers—what do they round
    your door?
"They guard our master's granaries from the thin hands
    of the poor."
Pale mothers, wherefore weeping? "Would to God that
    we were dead—
Our children swoon before us, and we cannot give them
    bread!"

Little children, tears are strange upon your infant faces,
God meant you but to smile within your mother's soft
    embraces.
"Oh! we know not what is smiling, and we know not
    what is dying;
But we're hungry, very hungry, and we cannot stop
    our crying.
And some of us grow cold and white—we know not what
    it means;
But as they lie beside us we tremble in our dreams."
There's a gaunt crowd on the highway—are you come to
    pray to man,
With hollow eyes that cannot weep, and for words your
    faces wan?

"No; the blood is dead within our veins—we care not
    now for life;
Let us die hid in the ditches, far from children and
    from wife!

We cannot stay to listen to their raving famished cries—
Bread! Bread! Bread! and none to still their agonies.
We left an infant playing with her dead mother's hand:
We left a maiden maddened by the fever's scorching
      brand:"
Better, maiden, thou wert strangled in thy own dark-
      twisted tresses!
Better, infant, thou wert smothered in thy mother's
      first caresses.

"We are fainting in our misery, but God will hear our
      groan;
Yet, if fellow-men desert us, will He hearken from His
      throne?
Accursed are we in our own land, yet toil we still and
      toil;
But the stranger reaps our harvest—the alien owns our
      soil.
O Christ! how have we sinned, that on our native plains
We perish homeless, naked, starved, with branded brow
      like Cain's?
Dying, dying wearily, with a torture sure and slow—
Dying as a dog would die, by the wayside as we go.

"One by one they're falling round us, their pale faces
      to the sky;
We've no strength left to dig them graves—there let
      them lie.
The wild bird, if he's stricken, is mourned by the others,
But we—we die in Christian land,—we die amid our
      brothers,
In the land which God has given, like a wild beast in
      his cave,
Without a tear, a prayer, a shroud, a coffin, or a grave.
Ha! but think ye the contortions on each livid face
      ye see,
Will not be read on Judgment-day by eyes of Deity?

"We are wretches, famished, scorned, human tools to
    build your pride,
But God will yet take vengeance for the souls for whom
    Christ died.
Now is your hour of pleasure—bask ye in the world's
    caress;
But our whitening bones against ye will rise as witnesses,
From the cabins and the ditches in their charred,
    uncoffined masses,
For the Angel of the Trumpet will know them as he
    passes.
A ghastly spectral army, before great God we'll stand,
And arraign ye as our murderers, O spoilers of our
    land!"

LADY WILDE (SPERANZA)

THE EXODUS

"A million a decade!" Calmly and cold
  The units are read by our statesmen sage;
Little they think of a nation old,
  Fading away from history's page;
    Outcast weeds by a desolate sea—
    Fallen leaves of humanity.

"A million a decade!"—of human wrecks,
  Corpses lying in fever sheds—
Corpses huddled on foundering decks,
  And shroudless dead on their rocky beds;
    Nerve and muscle, and heart and brain,
    Lost to Ireland—lost in vain.

"A million a decade!" Count ten by ten,
  Column and line of the record fair;
Each unit stands for ten thousand men,

153

Staring with blank, dead eye-balls there
　　Strewn like blasted trees on the sod,
　　Men that were made in the image of God.

"A million a decade!"—and nothing done;
　　The Caesars had less to conquer a world;
And the war for the right not yet begun,
　　The banner of freedom not yet unfurled;
　　　The soil is fed by the weed that dies;
　　　If forest leaves fall, yet they fertilize.

But ye—dead, dead, not climbing the height,
　　Not clearing a path for the future to tread;
Not opening the golden portals of light,
　　Ere the gate was choked by your piled-up dead:
　　　Martyrs ye, yet never a name
　　　Shines on the golden roll of fame.

Had ye rent one gyve of the festering chain,
　　Strangling the life of the nation's soul;
Poured your life-blood by river and plain,
　　Yet touched with your dead hand freedom's goal;
　　　Left of heroes one footprint more
　　　On our soil, tho' stamped in your gore—

We could triumph while mourning the brave,
　　Dead for all that was holy and just,
And write, through our tears, on the grave,
　　As we flung down the dust to dust—
　　　"They died for their country, but led
　　　Her up from the sleep of the dead."

"A million a decade!" What does it mean?
　　A nation dying of inner decay—
A churchyard silence where life has been—
　　The base of the pyramid crumbling away:
　　　A drift of men gone over the sea,
　　　A drift of the dead where men should be.

Was it for this ye plighted your word,
  Crowned and crownless rulers of men?
Have ye kept faith with your crucified Lord,
  And fed his sheep till he comes again?
    Or fled like hireling shepherds away,
    Leaving the fold the gaunt wolf's prey?

Have ye given of your purple to cover,
  Have ye given of your gold to cheer,
Have ye given of your love, as a lover
  Might cherish the bride he held dear,
    Broken the sacrament-bread to feed
    Souls and bodies in uttermost need?

Ye stand at the judgment-bar to-day—
  The angels are counting the dead-roll, too;
Have ye trod in the pure and perfect way,
  And ruled for God as the crowned should do?
    Count our dead—before angels and men,
    Ye're judged and doomed by the statist's pen.

After visiting workhouses in famine areas in 1849, Thomas Carlyle wrote: "Human swinery has here reached its acme. Can it be charity to keep men alive on these terms? In face of all the twaddle of the earth, shoot a man rather than train him (with heavy expense to his neighbors) to be a deceptive human swine." When asked for alms by starving beggars, Carlyle told them: "Wouldn't it be worth your consideration, whether you hadn't better drown or hang yourselves, than live a dog's life in this way?" He summed up his opinion of the Irish peasants: "No hope for the men as masters; their one true station in the universe is servants, 'slaves' if you will. They are, in brief, dark barbarians not intrinsically of ill dispositions."
After the potato famine, British landlords in Ireland began evicting farmers and turning their fields over to large-scale grazing of cattle. According to official British records, in the thirty-

three years from 1849 to 1882 the number of families evicted totaled 482,000. Mrs. Seumas MacManus (1866-1902) who wrote much poetry under the name Ethna Carbery, gives this touching picture of the situation.

Mrs. Seumas MacManus (Ethna Carbery)

THE PASSING OF THE GAEL

They are going, going, going from the valleys and the
      hills,
They are leaving far behind them heathery moor and
      mountain rills,
All the wealth of hawthorn hedges where the brown
      thrush sways and trills.

They are going, shy-eyed colleens and the lads so straight
      and tall,
From the purple peaks of Kerry, from the crags of wild
      Imaal,
From the greening plains of Mayo and the glens of
      Donegal.

They are leaving pleasant places, shores with snowy
      sands outspread;
Blue and lonely lakes a-stirring when the wind stirs
      overhead;
Tender living hearts that love them, and the graves of
      kindred dead.

They shall carry to the distant land a tear-drop in the
      eye,
And some shall go uncomforted—their days an endless
      sigh
For Kathaleen Ni Houlihan's sad face, until they die.

156

Oh, Kathaleen Ni Houlihan, your road's a thorny way,
And 'tis a faithful soul would walk the flints with you
for aye,
Would walk the sharp and cruel flints until his locks
grew gray.

So some must wander to the East, and some must wander
West;
Some seek the white wastes of the North, and some a
Southern nest:
Yet never shall they sleep so sweet as on your mother
breast.

The whip of hunger scourged them from the glens and
quiet moors,
But there's a hunger of the heart that plenty never
cures;
And they shall pine to walk again the rough road that
is yours.

Within the city streets, hot, hurried, full of care,
A sudden dream shall bring them a whiff of Irish air—
A cool air, faintly-scented, blown soft from otherwhere.

Oh, the cabins long-deserted! (Olden memories awake)
Oh, the pleasant, pleasant places! Hush! The blackbird
in the brake!
Oh, the dear and kindly voices! (Now their hearts are
fain to ache)

They may win a golden store—sure the whins were
golden too;
And no foreign skies hold beauty like the rainy skies
they knew;
Nor any night-wind cool the brows as did the foggy dew.

.   .   .

They are going, going, going, and we cannot bid them
　　stay;
The fields are now the strangers' where the strangers'
　　cattle stray.
　*Oh! Kathaleen Ni Houlihan, your way's a thorny
　　way!*

LADY DUFFERIN

LAMENT OF THE IRISH EMIGRANT

I'm sittin' on the stile, Mary,
　Where we sat side by side,
On a bright May mornin', long ago,
　When first you were my bride:
The corn was springin' fresh and green,
　And the lark sang loud and high—
And the red was on your lip, Mary,
　And the lovelight in your eye.

The *place* is little changed, Mary;
　The day is bright as then;
The lark's loud song is in my ear,
　And the corn is green again;
But I miss the soft clasp of your hand,
　And your breath, warm on my cheek,
And I still keep list'nin' for the words
　You never more will speak.

'T is but a step down yonder lane,
　And the little church stands near—
The church where we were wed, Mary;
　I see the spire from here.
But the graveyard lies between, Mary,
　And my step might break your rest—
For I've laid you, darling! down to sleep
　With your baby on your breast.

I'm very lonely now, Mary,
  For the poor make no new friends:
But, oh! they love the better still,
  The few our Father sends!
And you were all *I* had, Mary—
  My blessin' and my pride!
There's nothin' left to care for now,
  Since my poor Mary died.

Yours was the good, brave heart, Mary,
  That still kept hoping on
When the trust in God had left my soul,
  And my arm's young strength was gone;
There was comfort ever on your lip
  And the kind look on your brow—
I bless you, Mary, for that same,
  Though you cannot hear me now.

I thank you for the patient smile
  When your heart was fit to break,
When the hunger-pain was gnawin' there,
  And you hid it for *my* sake;
I bless you for the pleasant word
  When your heart was sad and sore—
Oh! I'm thankful you are gone, Mary,
  Where grief can't reach you more!

I'm biddin' you a long farewell,
  My Mary—kind and true!
But I'll not forget *you*, darling,
  In the land I'm goin' to:
They say there's bread and work for all,
  And the sun shines always there—
But I'll not forget Old Ireland,
  Were it fifty times as fair!

And often in those grand old woods
  I'll sit and shut my eyes,
And my heart will travel back again
  To the place where Mary lies;
And I'll think I see the little stile
  Where we sat side by side,
And the springin' corn, and the bright May morn,
  When first you were my bride.

ELLEN FORESTER (1828-1883)

THE WIDOW'S MESSAGE TO HER SON

"Remember, Denis, all I bade you say;
  Tell him we're well and happy, thank the Lord;
But of our troubles, since he went away,
  You'll mind, *avick,* and never say a word!
    Of cares and troubles, sure, we've all our share;
    The finest summer isn't always fair.

"Tell him the spotted heifer calved in May;
  She died, poor thing; but that you needn't mind;
Nor how the constant rain destroyed the hay;
  But tell him God to us was ever kind;
    And when the fever spread the country o'er,
    His mercy kept the 'sickness' from our door.

"Be sure you tell him how the neighbors came
  And cut the corn; and stored it in the barn;
'T would be as well to mention them by name—
  Pat Murphy, Ned M'Cabe, and James M'Carn,
    And big Tim Daly from behind the hill;
    But say *agra* ¹—O say I miss him still!

---

¹ *Agradh:* O love!

"They came with ready hands our toil to share—
'T was then I missed him most—my own right hand;
I felt, although kind hearts were round me there,
The kindest heart beat in a foreign land.
Strong hand! brave heart! O severed far from me
By many a weary league of shore and sea!

"And tell him she was with us—he'll know who:
Mavourneen,[2] hasn't she the winsome eyes?
The darkest, deepest, brightest, bonniest blue,
I ever saw except in summer skies.
And such black hair! it is the blackest hair
That ever rippled over neck so fair.

"Tell him old Pincher fretted many a day
And moped, poor dog, 't was well he didn't die;
Crouched by the roadside, how he watched the way,
And sniffed the travelers as they passed him by—
Hail, rain, or sunshine, sure 't was all the same,
He listened for the foot that never came.

"Tell him the house is lonesome-like, and cold,
The fire itself seems robbed of half its light;
But maybe 't is my eyes are growing old,
And things look dim before my failing sight:
For all that, tell him 't was myself that spun
The shirts you bring, and stitched them every one.

"Give him my blessing, morning, noon, and night;
Tell him my prayers are offered for his good,
That he may keep his Maker still in sight,
And firmly stand, as his brave father stood,
True to his name, his country, and his God,
Faithful at home and steadfast still abroad."

---

[2] *Mo-húirnin:* my darling.

I'M VERY HAPPY WHERE I AM

I'm very happy where I am,
   Far across the say,
I'm very happy far from home,
   In North Amerikay.

It's lonely in the night, when Pat
   Is sleeping by my side,
I lie awake, and no one knows
   The big tears that I've cried.

For a little voice still calls me back
   To my far, far counthrie,
And nobody can hear it spake,
   O! nobody but me.

There is a little spot of ground
   Behind the chapel wall,
It's nothing but a tiny mound,
   Without a stone at all.

It rises like my heart just now,
   It makes a dawny hill;
It's from below the voice comes out,
   I cannot kape it still.

O! Little Voice, ye call me back
   To my far, far counthrie,
And nobody can hear ye spake,
   O! nobody but me.

THE IRISH PEASANT GIRL

Charles Joseph Kickham (1830-1882) lost his hearing while a boy, lost his sight while in prison as a Fenian leader, and wrote Knocknagow, *probably the most continuously and widely beloved Irish novel. Previous novels had dealt with the upper classes, Irish and Anglo-Irish, with the peasants depicted as buffoons. Kickham's ballads also had a wide appeal.*

She lived beside the Anner,
At the foot of Slievna-man,
A gentle peasant girl,
With mild eyes like the dawn;
Her lips were dewy rosebuds;
Her teeth of pearls rare;
And a snow-drift 'neath a beechen bough
Her neck and nut-brown hair.

How pleasant 'twas to meet her
On Sunday, when the bell
Was filling with its mellow tones
Lone wood and grassy dell
And when at eve young maidens
Strayed the river bank along,
The widow's brown-haired daughter
Was loveliest of the throng.

O brave, brave Irish girls—
We well may call you brave!—
Sure the least of all your perils
Is the stormy ocean wave,
When you leave our quiet valleys,
And cross the Atlantic's foam,
To hoard your hard-won earnings
For the helpless ones at home.

"Write word to my own dear mother—
Say, we'll meet with God above;
And tell my little brothers
I send them all my love;
May the angels ever guard them,
Is their dying sister's prayer"—
And folded in a letter
Was a braid of nut-brown hair.

Ah, cold and well-nigh callous,
This weary heart has grown
For thy helpless fate, dear Ireland,
And for sorrows of my own;
Yet a tear my eye will moisten,
When by Anner side I stray,
For the lily of the mountain foot
That withered far away.

Daniel O'Connell, one of the world's greatest orators and politicians, by peaceful means brought about Catholic Emancipation and initiated a movement for repeal of the Act of Union with England. When it became apparent that constitutional agitation would not bring home rule, a group known as Young Irelanders moved toward rebellion. They were inspired by the poets of The Nation, *a weekly newspaper, founded by Thomas Osborn Davis. Among these poets were Mangan, McCarthy, Ferguson, McGee, and Lady Wilde. Action was accelerated by the famine of 1846, when more food was exported by landlords than would have been ample to feed the thousands who died of starvation. O'Connell died in 1847, and in 1848 the Young Irelanders rebelled.*

After the revolt of 1848 had been crushed, many rebels were convicted of treason. Some were sentenced to be hanged, drawn, and quartered, others to prison, and others to transportation to distant penal colonies in Tasmania, then known as Van Diemen's Land. Twenty-three years later one of the rebels, Charles Gavan Duffy, became Premier of Australia. When Queen Victoria was asked by her Prime Minister to confer knighthood on him, she asked for a report on the other convicts of 1848. Here are some of the results:

Thomas Francis Meagher had escaped to America in 1852. Before his death in 1867 he became a general in the Union Army and raised the famous Irish Brigade that distinguished itself in the Civil War. At the time of his death he was Governor of Montana. Thirty-eight regiments in the Union Army had "Irish" in their names.

Before his death in 1868 Thomas D'Arcy McGee had become Minister of Agriculture of Canada and member of the Canadian Parliament.

Richard O'Gorman was Governor General of Newfoundland.

Morris Lyene was Attorney General of Australia, and was succeeded by another rebel, Michael Ireland.

John Mitchell was active in New York politics. His grandson, John Purroy Mitchell, became Mayor of New York.

Patrick Donahue was a brigadier general in the United States Army.

Timothy Daniel Sullivan had served as Lord Mayor of Dublin and had been three times elected to the British Parliament. He wrote the following popular song of Irish exiles, "Dear Old Ireland":

TIMOTHY DANIEL SULLIVAN (1827-1914)

DEAR OLD IRELAND

Deep in Canadian woods we've met,
　From one bright island flown;
Great is the land we tread, but yet
　Our hearts are with our own.
And ere we leave this shanty small,
　While fades the Autumn day,
　　We'll toast Old Ireland!
　　Dear Old Ireland!
　　Ireland, boys, hurrah!

We've heard her faults a hundred times,
  The new ones and the old,
In songs and sermons, ranns and rhymes,
  Enlarged some fifty-fold.
But take them all, the great and small,
  And this we've got to say:
    Here's dear Old Ireland!
    Good Old Ireland!
    Ireland, boys, hurrah!

And happy and bright are the groups that pass
  From their peaceful homes, for miles
O'er fields and roads and hills, to Mass,
  When Sunday morning smiles;
And deep the zeal their true hearts feel
  When low they kneel and pray.
    Oh, dear Old Ireland!
    Blest Old Ireland!
    Ireland, boys, hurrah!

But deep in the Canadian woods we've met,
  And we never may see again
The dear old isle where our hearts are set
  And our first fond hopes remain!
But come, fill up another cup,
  And with every sup we'll say,
    "Here's dear Old Ireland!
    Loved Old Ireland!
    Ireland, boys, hurrah!

We know that brave and good men tried
  To snap her rusty chain—
That patriots suffered, martyrs died—
  And all, 'tis said, in vain.
But no, boys, no! a glance will show
  How far they've won their way—
    Here's good Old Ireland!
    Brave Old Ireland!
    Ireland, boys, hurrah!

We've seen the wedding and the wake,
  The patron and the fair;
And lithe young frames at the dear old games
  In the kindly Irish air;
And the loud "hurroo," we have heard it too,
  And the thundering "Clear the way!"
    Here's gay Old Ireland!
    Dear Old Ireland!
    Ireland, boys, hurrah!

And well we know in the cool gray eves,
  When the hard day's work is o'er,
How soft and sweet are the words that greet
  The friends who meet once more;
With "Mary machree!" "My Pat! 'tis he!"
  And "My own heart night and day!"
    Ah, fond Old Ireland!
    Dear Old Ireland!
    Ireland, boys, hurrah!

In *"The Winding Banks of Erne,"* William Allingham *wrote:*

Adieu to Ballyshannon! where I was bred and born;
Go where I may, I'll think of you as sure as night and
      morn,
The kindly spot, the friendly town where everyone is
      known,
And not a face in all the place but partly seems my own.
There's not a house or window, there's not a field or
      hill,
But east or west, in foreign lands, I'll recollect them
      still,
I leave my warm heart with you, though my back I'm
      forced to turn—
So, adieu to Ballyshannon and the winding banks of
      Erne.

Kipling has Private Terence Mulvaney lamenting from his barracks in India:

> *Eyah! Cork's own city an' the blue sky above ut—*
> *An' the times that was—the times that was.*

JOHN LOCKE

THE EXILE'S RETURN, OR MORNING ON THE IRISH COAST

John Locke (1847-1889) began writing revolutionary poems when only sixteen years old. He continued to write them while in Kilkenny prison, and after being banished to New York. He was a friend of my ancestors in County Tipperary.

> *Th' anám an Dhia.* But there it is—
>   The dawn on the hills of Ireland!
> God's angels lifting the night's black veil
>   From the fair, sweet face of my sireland!
> O Ireland isn't it grand you look—
>   Like a bride in her rich adornin'?
> And with all the pent-up love of my heart
>   I bid you the top o' the mornin'!
>
> This one short hour pays lavishly back
>   For many a year of mourning;
> I'd almost venture another flight,
>   There's so much joy in returning—
> Watching out for the hallowed shore,
>   All other attractions scornin':
> O Ireland! don't you hear me shout?
>   I bid you the top o' the mornin'.
>
> Ho, ho! upon Cleena's shelving strand
>   The surges are grandly beating,
> And Kerry is pushing her headlands out
>   To give us the kindly greeting;

In to the shore the seabirds fly
  On pinions that know no drooping,
And out of the cliffs, with welcomes charged,
  A million of waves come trooping.

O kindly, generous, Irish land
  So leal and fair and loving!
No wonder the wandering Celt should think
  And dream of you in his roving.
The alien home may have gems and gold
  Shadows may never have gloomed it;
But the heart will sigh for the absent land
  Where the love-light first illumed it.

And doesn't old Cove look charming there,
  Watching the wild waves' motion,
Leaning her back up against the hills,
  And the tip of her toes in the ocean?
I wonder I don't hear Shandon's bells—
  Ah! maybe their chiming's over,
For it's many a year since I began
  The life of a Western rover.

Now fuller and truer the shore line shows—
  Was ever a scene so splendid!
I feel the breath of the Munster breeze;
  Thank God that my exile's ended!
Old scenes, old songs, old friends again,
  The vale and the cot I was born in—
O Ireland! up from my heart of hearts
  I bid you the top o' the mornin'!

JOSEPH I. C. CLARKE

THE FIGHTING RACE

*The United States' war with Spain in 1898 was triggered by
the sinking of the battleship* Maine *in Havana harbor. The list*

of men lost in that disaster inspired a New York newspaper editor, Joseph I. C. Clarke (1846-1925) to write a poem which he entitled "The Fighting Race," but which is better known as "Kelly and Burke and Shea."

"Read out the names!" and Burke sat back,
   And Kelly drooped his head,
While Shea—they call him Scholar Jack—
   Went down the list of the dead.
Officers, seamen, gunners, marines,
   The crews of the gig and yawl,
The bearded man and the lad in his teens,
   Carpenters, coal passers—all.
Then, knocking the ashes from out his pipe,
   Said Burke in an offhand way:
"We're all in that dead man's list, by Cripe!
   Kelly and Burke and Shea."
"Well, here's to the Maine, and I'm sorry for Spain,"
   Said Kelly and Burke and Shea.

"Wherever there's Kellys there's trouble," said Burke.
   "Wherever fighting's the game,
Or a spice of danger in grown man's work,"
   Said Kelly, "you'll find my name."
"And do we fall short," said Burke, getting mad,
   "When it's touch and go for life?"
Said Shea, "It's thirty-odd years, bedad,
   Since I charged to drum and fife
Up Marye's Heights, and my old canteen
   Stopped a rebel ball on its way.
There were blossoms of blood on our sprigs of green—
   Kelly and Burke and Shea—
And the dead didn't brag." "Well, here's to the flag!"
   Said Kelly and Burke and Shea.

"I wish 'twas in Ireland, for there's the place,"
   Said Burke, "that we'd die by right,
In the cradle of our soldier race,
   After one good stand-up fight.

My grandfather fell on Vinegar Hill,
  And fighting was not his trade;
But his rusty pike's in the cabin still,
  With Hessian blood on the blade."
"Aye, aye," said Shea, "the pikes were great
  When the word was 'clear the way!' "
We were thick on the roll in ninety-eight—
  Kelly and Burke and Shea."
"Well, here's to the pike and the sword and the like!"
  Said Kelly and Burke and Shea.

And Shea, the scholar, with rising joy,
  Said, "We were at Ramillies.
We left our bones at Fontenoy
  And up in the Pyrenees.
Before Dunkirk, on Landen's plain,
  Cremona, Lille and Ghent,
We're all over Austria, France and Spain,
  Wherever they pitched a tent.
We've died for England from Waterloo
  To Egypt and Dargai;
And still there's enough for a corps or a crew,
  Kelly and Burke and Shea."
"Well, here is to good honest fighting blood!"
  Said Kelly and Burke and Shea.

"Oh, the fighting races don't die out,
  If they seldom die in bed,
For love is first in their hearts, no doubt,"
  Said Burke; then Kelly said:
"When Michael, the Irish Archangel, stands,
  The angel with the sword,
And the battle-dead from a hundred lands
  Are ranged in one big horde,
Our line, that for Gabriel's trumpet waits,
  Will stretch three deep that day,
From Jehoshaphat to the Golden Gates—
  Kelly and Burke and Shea."
"Well, here's thank God for the race and the sod!"
  Said Kelly and Burke and Shea.

In the spring of 1918 General Pershing launched his great offensive of the First World War. On April 11 The Chicago Tribune *printed the names of 265 American soldiers killed or wounded. It was the longest such list since the Civil War more than half a century earlier. Of the 265 casualties more than a hundred bore Irish names: Barry, Casey, Callahan, Kelly, Murphy, Mulcahy, McCabe, McCormack, McKenna, McMahon, McNamara, O'Brien, O'Connor, O'Gorman, O'Keefe, O'Neill, O'Rourke, Ryan, Sullivan, Walsh, etc. In World War II the first American mother to lose five sons was Mrs. Thomas P. Sullivan. Other heroes of World War II were William P. O'Brien, first American pilot to bomb Berlin; Lieutenant Colonel Michael Murphy, pilot of the first American glider to land on D-day; Lieutenant John F. Murphy, first to land on Bataan; Colin Kelly; "Wild Bill" Donovan; and Father Duffy.*

REV. J. B. DOLLARD   (1872-1946)

THE "CELTIC FRINGE"

These verses were written during World War II by a Canadian priest.

Remnant of a scattered people—
Munsters, Leinsters, Connaught Rangers;
Ye who held at Mons the rear guard,
Ye who waded in at Suvla,
When the scythe of Death was glutted!
Ye who brought relief at Langemarck,
Now ye hold the ravened Bulgar,
Hold the Teuton, hold the Moslem,
While your allies bring their forces
Safe from out the jaws of danger;
Once again ye show the nations
Love surpassing love of woman,
Laying down your lives for others!

Long ye went unprized, uncherished,
With your Celtic Highland brothers,
Poverty your constant comrade;
Ever goaded into exile,
Filling all the seas and oceans
With your tears and with your bodies!
(All unprized, the Celtic clansmen
Fled to foreign shores in myriads,
Left their faery glens forsaken!)

Munsters, Leinsters, Connaught Rangers,
Black Watch, Seaforths, Cameronians,
Men of Hebrides and Orkney—
O, for millions of such heroes,
Lost through exile and through famine,
Lost because of statesmen's blunders,
Lost because of tongues of evil
Spreading hatred and division
'Twixt the banded British peoples!

Nevermore can they ignore ye,
Munsters, Leinsters, Connaught Rangers,
Seaforths, Black Watch, Cameronians!
See the foe, amazed, affrighted,
Quails before your charging slogan!
Ye have won unfading glory.
Lo! the nations sound your praises.
Lo! the "Celtic Fringe" derided,
Fringes round the empire's armies
With a fringe of fire and valor!

May that fringe for aye grow stronger,
Till the Celt (who dies for Freedom)
Bulwarks all the little peoples
'Gainst the might of leagued Oppression,
'Gainst the menace of the Tyrant,
'Gainst the plots of knaves and madmen!

THE IRISH

Have you heard of a Little People, who hail from a
    Little Isle,
Where the Shamrock grows in the meadow and the
    colleen waits by the stile?
Have you heard of My Little People, as they wander to
    and fro
In the lands of their Love and Labor where the Irish
    exiles go!
They builded the great West railroads,
   And limbered the world's great guns;
They'll follow the last o' the trail roads
   Wherever the last trail runs.

They are gentle in peace, my kinsfolk, but somewhat
    averse in strife,
Having learned in their early conflicts the value of
    that called—Life.
They are lions and doves together; together they laugh
    and cry—
But no man says of the Irish that they know not how
    to die.
For their Soggarth stands before them,
   And he bids the ranks to kneel,
When the war smoke thickens o'er them
   And the muzzles click to steel.

They play them a step of music; 'tis maybe a rebel tune
Of the pike on an Irish shoulder at the rise of an Irish
    moon—
The tears on the Colonel's features are terribly sad
    to see,
But nobody asks their reason—excepting the enemy.
They fight for the Kings of Britain,
   They fight for the Queens of Spain;

But Czar, nor Kaiser, nor Sultan,
  Has called them ever in vain.

They rode with the Little Captain at Jena and Waterloo;
They walked with their ancient foreman a'shoulder at
          Tugela, too!
They are gentle in peace, my kinsmen, but surely the
          World-at-Large
Must clear the way for the Irish, when the Irish call
          the "charge."
Oh, the smell of the battle powder,
  Is a savour sweet to the Celt,
When the kettle-drums rattle louder
  In the heart of the firing belt.

So, not with a song of boasting; and not with a song
          of pride,
I am glad of my Little People who wandered, and fought
          and died.
They salted the Earth with their courage,
          and filled the Earth with their strength,
And the God of their Irish mothers will answer
          their prayers at length.
Wherever the Wild Folk wander,
  Wherever the Kind Folk bide,
The Faith and the Hope is in them
  Whatever, whate'er, betide.

Ye will hear of the Little People who hail from the
          Western Isle,
Where the Shamrock grows in the meadow,
          and the colleen waits by the stile,
Ye will hear of my Irish people—'till the work of the
          world shall cease—
In the fields of the Nations' battles, in the halls
          of the Empires' peace.

THE IRISH DEAD

The Irish Dead—in their thousands they sleep in the
      Emerald Isle—
Men who died thinking of Ireland and, thinking, died
      with a smile.
Like Emmet, they had no epitaphs; their very graves
      unknown,
With palace and rath and battlefield under the grass
      upgrown.
But the shamrock is their mourning wreath; Erin's
      soft rain the tears
That ceaselessly weep the gallant dead of Ireland's
      thousand years,
And the Round Towers stand as monuments to the far-
      off men who led
In the dim and distant ages the legion of Irish Dead.

The Irish Dead—in their thousands they sleep on the
      stricken fields,
Where they fell under alien banners with the courage
      that never yields.
And the foeman "remembered Limerick" wherever the
      Wild Geese flew,
The fiercest, most daring fighters that ever the old world
      knew.
Unmarked are their graves, but the nations remember
      the Irish name
And the Irish note that is blown on the battle-trumpet
      of fame.
While Valor, dropping her swordpoint, dreams with
      down-bowed head
Of the valorous sons that she numbered in the legion
      of Irish Dead.

The Irish Dead—in their thousands they sleep in their
      quiet graves,

Some in the land that bore them, some in countries
        beyond the waves;
But the shamrock still is springing from the soil of the
        Emerald Isle,
And the living sons of Ireland see the vales of Ireland
        smile.
So we drink a toast to the future, as we proudly think of
        the past,
To Ireland, the crownless nation, that comes to her
        own at last.
Salute the spirit of Erin, proclaiming with upraised head
That her sons will be worthy of Ireland and the legion
        of Irish Dead.

REBELLION

Poems inspired by, and to inspire, rebellion against English rule are many. None was more loved and quoted than "The Memory of the Dead." It was written about 1840 by John Kells Ingram (1823-1907) while he was a student at Trinity College, a bulwark of Anglican supremacy. It was printed anonymously and became the inspiration of Irish rebels at home and abroad —Repealers, Fenians, Clan na Gael, Sinn Feiners. In the meantime the author became a conservative professor and government official, changed his mind about Irish independence, and did not acknowledge authorship until he was seventy years old.

JOHN KELLS INGRAM

THE MEMORY OF THE DEAD (1798)

Who fears to speak of Ninety-Eight?
   Who blushes at the name?
When cowards mock the patriot's fate,
   Who hangs his head for shame?
He's all a knave, or half a slave,
   Who slights his country thus;
But a true man, like you, man,
   Will fill your glass with us.

We drink the memory of the brave,
　The faithful and the few:
Some lie afar beyond the wave,
　Some sleep in Ireland, too;
All, all are gone; but still lives on
　The fame of those who died;
All true men, like you men,
　Remember them with pride.

Some on the shores of distant lands
　Their weary hearts have laid,
And by the stranger's heedless hands
　Their lonely graves were made;
But, though their clay be far away
　Beyond the Atlantic foam,
In true men, like you men,
　Their spirit's still at home.

The dust of some is Irish earth,
　Among their own they rest,
And the same land that gave them birth
　Has caught them to her breast;
And we will pray that from their clay
　Full many a race may start
Of true men, like you men,
　To act as brave a part.

They rose in dark and evil days
　To right their native land;
They kindled there a living blaze
　That nothing shall withstand.
Alas! That Might can vanquish Right—
　They fell and passed away;
But true men, like you men,
　Are plenty here today.

Then here's their memory—may it be
　For us a guiding light,
To cheer our strife for liberty,

And teach us to unite—
Through good and ill, be Ireland's still,
Though sad as theirs your fate,
And true men be you, men,
Like those of Ninety-Eight.

The most widely known Irish song is "The Wearing of the Green," originally a street ballad dating from the revolt of 1798. Dion Boucicault, noted composer, playwright, and actor, rewrote it for his play Arrah na Pogue. *It was first sung in London on March 22, 1865, and almost caused a riot as Clerkenwell Prison had recently been blown up by Fenians. Queen Victoria asked her Cabinet to issue an edict that it must never again be sung in British dominions.*

In spite of this prohibition (or because of it), the song became popular around the globe. It was not publicly heard for many years in England, but when Queen Victoria visited Ireland in 1900 she was greeted with great choruses singing "The Wearing of the Green."

*Oh, Paddy dear, and did ye hear the news that's goin'
    round?*
    *The shamrock is by law forbid to grow on Irish
        ground!*
*St. Patrick's day no more we'll keep; his color can't be
    seen,*
    *For there's a cruel law ag'in' the Wearin' o' the
        Green!*
*I met with Napper Tandy, and he took me by the hand,
    And he said, "How's poor ould Ireland, and how does
        she stand?"*
*She's the most distressful country that ever yet was seen,
    For they're hanging men and women there for the
        Wearin' o' the Green.*

*So if the color we must wear is England's cruel red,
    Let it remind us of the blood that Irishmen have shed.*

180

You may take the shamrock from your hat, and cast it
      on the sod,
   But never fear, 'twill take root there, though under
      foot 'tis trod.
When law can stop the blades of grass from growin' as
      they grow,
   An' when the trees in summer time their color dare
      not show,
Then I will change the color, too, I wear in my caubeen;
   But till that day, plaise God, I'll stick to the Wearin'
      o' the Green.

Napper Tandy (1740-1803) was an Irish revolutionist who
attempted to help the rebellion in America by preventing the
use of English goods in Ireland. When about to be tried for
seditious writing, he escaped to America and then to France,
where he was put in charge of a vessel for the invasion of Ireland.
He was condemned to death by the British and made a general
by Napoleon.

Dion Boucicault wrote this third verse which has long since
been discarded:

But if at last our color should be torn from Ireland's
      heart,
   Her sons with shame and sorrow from the dear old isle
      will part.
I've heard whisper of a country that lies beyond the sea
   Where rich and poor stand equal in the light of
      freedom's day.
O Erin must we leave you, driven by a tyrant's hand?
   Must we ask a mother's blessing from a strange and
      distant land?
Where the cruel cross of England shall never more be
      seen,
   And where, please God, we'll live and die still wearing
      of the green.

The first verse of "The Wearing of the Green" was translated into Latin by M. D. Forrest as follows:

Audistine, carissime, quid ferant undique?
   Hibernia trifolium vetatur crescere;
Patricium non amplius colemus splendide,
   Nam lux crudelis prohibet gestare viride.
Napperio locutus sum, qyi tensa dextra
   Quaesivit de Hibernis et dilecta patria:
Cum viros atque feminas trucident, regio
   Est omnium miserrima a mundo condito.

THOMAS MOORE

THE MINSTREL BOY

The minstrel boy to the war is gone,
   In the ranks of death you'll find him,
His father's sword he has girded on,
   And his wild harp slung behind him.
"Land of song!" said the warrior bard,
   "Though all the world betrays thee,
One sword, at least, thy rights shall guard,
   One faithful harp shall praise thee!"

The minstrel fell!—but the foeman's chain
   Could not bring his proud soul under;
The harp he loved ne'er spoke again,
   For he tore its chords asunder;
And said, "No chains shall sully thee,
   Thou soul of love and bravery!
Thy songs were made for the pure and free,
   They shall never sound in slavery!"

LAMENT FOR THE DEATH OF OWEN ROE O'NEILL

Time—10th November, 1649. Scene—Ormond's Camp, Co. Waterford. Speakers—a Veteran of Eoghan O'Neill's clan, and one of the horsemen just arrived with an account of his death.

"Did they dare, did they dare, to slay Eoghan Ruadh
  O'Neill?"
"Yes, they slew with poison him they feared to meet with
  steel."
"May God wither up their hearts! May their blood cease
  to flow!
May they walk in living death, who poisoned Eoghan
  Ruadh!

"Though it break my heart to hear, say again the bitter
  words."
"From Derry, against Cromwell, he marched to measure
  swords;
But the weapon of the Sacsanach met him on his way,
And he died at Clough Aughter, upon Saint Leonard's
  day."

"Wail, wail ye for the Mighty One! Wail, wail ye for
  the Dead;
Quench the hearth, and hold the breath—with ashes
  strew the head.
How tenderly we loved him! How deeply we deplore!
Holy Saviour! but to think we shall never see him more!

"Sagest in the council was he, kindest in the Hall:
Sure we never won a battle—'twas Eoghan won them all.
Had he lived—had he lived—our dear country had been
  free;
But he's dead, but he's dead, and 'tis slaves we'll ever be.

"O'Farrell and Clanricard, Preston and Red Hugh,
Audley and MacMahon—ye are valiant, wise, and true;
But—what, what are ye all to our darling who is gone?
The Rudder of our ship was he, our Castle's corner-stone!

"Wail, wail him through the Island! Weep, weep for our
         pride!
Would that on the battle-field our gallant chief had died!
Weep the Victor of Benburb—weep him, young man
         and old;
Weep for him, ye women—your Beautiful lies cold!

"We thought you would not die—we were sure you
         would not go,
And leave us in our utmost need to Cromwell's cruel
         blow—
Sheep without a shepherd, when the snow shuts out the
         sky—
Oh! why did you leave us, Eoghan? Why did you die?

"Soft as woman's was your voice, O'Neill! bright was your
         eye,
Oh! why did you leave us, Eoghan? why did you die?
Your troubles are all over, you're at rest with God on
         high;
But we're slaves, and we're orphans, Eoghan!—why did
         you die?"

MICHAEL JOSEPH McCANN

O'DONNELL ABOO

*Michael Joseph McCann (1824-1883) wrote "O'Donnell Aboo"
while he was a professor at St. Jarlath's College, Tuam. Later he
was a journalist in London.*

Proudly the note of the trumpet is sounding,
Loudly the war-cries arise on the gale;
Fleetly the steed by Lough Swilly is bounding,
To join the thick squadrons in Saimear's green vale.
    On, ev'ry mountaineer,
    Strangers to flight and fear!
Rush to the standard of dauntless Red Hugh!
    Bonnaught and gallowglass,
    Throng from each mountain pass;
On for old Erin, "O'Donnell Aboo!"

Princely O'Neill to our aid is advancing
With many a chieftain and warrior clan,
A thousand proud steeds in his vanguard are prancing
'Neath the borderers brave from the banks of the Bann;
    Many a heart shall quail
    Under its coat of mail;
Deeply the merciless foeman shall rue,
    When on his ear shall ring,
    Borne on the breezes' wing,
Tir Connell's dread warcry, "O'Donnell Aboo!"

Wildly o'er Desmond the war-wolf is howling,
Fearless the eagle sweeps over the plain,
The fox in the streets of the city is prowling;
All, all who would scare them are banished or slain.
    Grasp every stalwart hand
    Hackbut and battle brand,
Pay them all back the debt so long due;
    Norris and Clifford well
    Can of Tir Connell tell;
Onward to glory, "O'Donnell Aboo!"

Sacred the cause of Clan Connaill's defending,
The altars we kneel at, the homes of our sires;
Ruthless the ruin the foe is extending,
Midnight is red with the plunderers' fires.
    On with O'Donnell, then,
    Fight the old fight again,

Sons of Tir Connell, all valiant and true.
  Make the false Saxon feel
  Erin's avenging steel!
Strike for your country, "O'Donnell Aboo!"

JOHN TODHUNTER

AGHADOE

There's a glade in Aghadoe, Aghadoe, Aghadoe,
There's a green and silent glade in Aghadoe,
  Where we met, my Love and I, Love's fair planet in
      the sky,
O'er that sweet and silent glade in Aghadoe.

There's a glen in Aghadoe, Aghadoe, Aghadoe,
There's a deep and secret glen in Aghadoe,
  Where I hid him from the eyes of the red-coats and
      their spies
That year the trouble came to Aghadoe.

Oh! my curse on one black heart in Aghadoe, Aghadoe,
On Shaun Dhuv, my mother's son in Aghadoe,
  When your throat fries in hell's drouth salt the flame
      be in your mouth,
For the treachery you did in Aghadoe!

For they tracked me to that glen in Aghadoe, Aghadoe,
When the price was on his head in Aghadoe;
  O'er the mountain through the wood, as I stole to him
      with food,
When in hiding lone he lay in Aghadoe.

But they never took him living in Aghadoe, Aghadoe;
With the bullets in his heart in Aghadoe,
  There he lay, the head—my breast keeps the warmth
      where once 'twould rest—
Gone, to win the traitor's gold from Aghadoe!

I walked to Mallow Town from Aghadoe, Aghadoe,
Brought his head from the gaol's gate to Aghadoe,
  Then I covered him with fern, and I piled on him the
     cairn,
Like an Irish king he sleeps in Aghadoe.

Oh, to creep into that cairn in Aghadoe, Aghadoe!
There to rest upon his breast in Aghadoe!
  Sure your dog for you could die with no truer heart
     than I—
Your own love cold on your cairn in Aghadoe.

ANONYMOUS

THE SHAN VAN VOCHT

*After the rebellions of 1798 and 1803 the Irish began to sing
and declaim in the streets patriotic verse such as "The Shan
Van Vocht," "The Wearing of the Green," and "The Memory
of the Dead." They had no newspapers or other publications
through which to express themselves. The ballads and poems
were printed on sheets and sold for a penny. In the 1830's the
British Parliament passed a law making such sale a criminal
act. Daniel O'Connell then instructed the vendors to carry a
handful of straw and to call out: "I'll sell you a straw for a
penny and make you a present of a song." This song was written
when the French fleet sailed for Ireland in 1796; but like the
Spanish Armada, the fleet was scattered by a storm and but few
ships entered Bantry Bay. Shan Van Vocht means "poor old
woman," i.e., Ireland.*

    Oh! the French are on the sea,
      Says the Shan Van Vocht;
    The French are on the sea,
      Says the Shan Van Vocht;
    Oh! the French are in the Bay,
    They'll be here without delay,

And the Orange will decay,
  Says the Shan Van Vocht.
    Oh! the French are in the Bay,
    They'll be here by break of day,
    And the Orange will decay,
      Says the Shan Van Vocht.

And where will they have their camp?
  Says the Shan Van Vocht;
Where will they have their camp?
  Says the Shan Van Vocht;
On the Curragh of Kildare,
The boys they will be there,
With their pikes in good repair,
  Says the Shan Van Vocht.
    To the Curragh of Kildare
    The boys they will repair,
    And Lord Edward will be there,
      Says the Shan Van Vocht.

Then what will the yeomen do?
  Says the Shan Van Vocht;
What will the yeomen do?
  Says the Shan Van Vocht;
What should the yeomen do
But throw off the Red and Blue,
And swear that they'll be true
    To the Shan Van Vocht?
    What should the yeomen do
    But throw off the Red and Blue,
    And swear that they'll be true
      To the Shan Van Vocht?

And what colour will they wear?
  Says the Shan Van Vocht;
What colour will they wear?
  Says the Shan Van Vocht;
What colour should be seen
Where our fathers' homes have been,

But our own immortal Green?
  Says the Shan Van Vocht.
    What colour should be seen
    Where our fathers' homes have been,
    But our own immortal Green?
    Says the Shan Van Vocht.

And will Ireland then be free?
  Says the Shan Van Vocht;
Will Ireland then be free?
  Says the Shan Van Vocht;
Yes! Ireland shall be free,
From the centre to the sea;
Then hurrah for Liberty!
  Says the Shan Van Vocht.
    Yes! Ireland shall be free,
    From the centre to the sea;
    Then hurrah for Liberty!
    Says the Shan Van Vocht.

KEVIN T. BUGGY

THE SAXON SHILLING

When an Irishman accepted a shilling from a recruiting offi-cer he was automatically enlisted in the British Army. Many a fellow took a few drinks and awoke to find "the Queen's shil-ling" in his pocket and her colors pinned to his coat. Kevin T. Buggy (1816-1843), a member of the London bar who succeeded Sir Charles Gavan Duffy as editor of The Belfast Vindicator, *wrote this popular poem shortly before his death in 1843.*

Hark! a martial sound is heard—
The march of soldiers, fifing, drumming;
Eyes are staring, hearts are stirred—
For bold recruits the brave are coming,
Ribands flaunting, feathers gay—

The sounds and sights are surely thrilling.
Dazzled village youths today
Will crowd to take the *Saxon Shilling*.

Ye whose spirits will not bow
In peace to parish tyrants longer—
Ye who wear the villain brow,
And ye who pine in hopeless hunger—
Fools without the brave man's faith—
All slaves and starvelings who are willing
To sell themselves to shame and death—
Accept the fatal *Saxon Shilling*.

Go—to find mid crime and toil,
The doom to which such guilt is hurried;
Go—to leave on Indian soil
Your bones to bleach, accursed, unburied!
Go—to crush the just and brave,
Whose wrongs with wrath the world is filling;
Go—to slay each brother slave
Or spurn the blood-stained *Saxon Shilling*.

Irish hearts! why should you bleed
To swell the tide of British glory—
Aiding despots in their need,
Who've changed our *green* so oft to *gory!*
None save those who wish to see
The noblest killed, the meanest killing,
And true hearts severed from the free,
Will take again the *Saxon Shilling*.

Irish youths! reserve your strength
Until an hour of glorious duty,
When Freedom's smile shall cheer at length
The land of bravery and beauty.
Bribes and threats, oh, heed no more—
Let nought but Justice make you willing
To leave your own dear Island shore,
For those who send the *Saxon Shilling*.

TIPPERARY RECRUITING SONG

'T is now we'd want to be wary, boys,
The recruiters are out in Tipperary, boys;
If they offer a glass, we'll wink as they pass—
We're old birds for chaff in Tipperary, boys.

Then, hurrah for the gallant Tipperary boys,
Although we're "cross and contrary," boys;
The never a one will handle a gun,
Except for the Green and Tipperary, boys,

Now mind what John Bull did here, my boys,
In the days of our famine and fear, my boys;
He burned and sacked, he plundered and racked,
Old Ireland of Irish to clear, my boys.

Now Bull wants to pillage and rob, my boys,
And put the proceeds in his fob, my boys;
But let each Irish blade just stick to his trade,
And let Bull do his own dirty job, my boys.

So never to 'list be in haste, my boys,
Or a glass of drugged whisky to taste, my boys;
If to India you go, it's to grief and to woe,
And to rot and to die like a beast, my boys.

But now he is beat for men, my boys,
His army is getting so thin, my boys,
With the fever and ague, the sword and the plague,
O, the devil a fear that he'll win, my boys.

Then mind not the nobblin' old schemer, boys,
Though he says that he's richer than Damer, boys;
Though he bully and roar, his power is o'er,
And his black heart will shortly be tamer, boys.

Now, isn't Bull peaceful and civil, boys,
In his mortal distress and his evil, boys?
But we'll cock each caubeen when his sergeants are
    seen,
And we'll tell them to go to the devil, boys.

Then hurrah for the gallant Tipperary boys!
Although "we're cross and contrary," boys;
The never a one will handle a gun,
Except for the Green and Tipperary, boys.

*Arthur Griffith wrote a poem about a Dublin boy who took
the English shilling and was mortally wounded by the Boers. Just
before he dies he says:*

*Yes, the curse of God is on me, an' I broke me mother's
    heart,*
*   An' me father's curse is on me, too, as well,*
*But wan thing cheers me still—when me life tonight I
    part*
I'll meet the man that 'listed me in hell.

*Thomas Carlyle, after his tour of Ireland in 1849, summed
up England's attitude as follows:*

*England does not hate you at all, nor love you at all;
merely values and will pay you according to the work
you can do.*

*Except for many generals and admirals, it is questionable
whether England adequately compensated the hundreds of
thousands of Irishmen who fought her battles all around the
world.*

PATRICK SHEEHAN

My name is Patrick Sheehan,
  My years are thirty-four;
Tipperary is my native place,
  Not far from Galtymore;
I came of honest parents,
  ·But now they're lying low;
And many a pleasant day I spent
  In the Glen of Aherlow.

I groped to find my musket—
  How dark I thought the night!
O blessed God, it was not dark,
  It was the broad daylight!
And when I found that I was *blind,*
  My tears began to flow;
I longed for even a pauper's grave
  In the Glen of Aherlow.

O blessed Virgin Mary,
  Mine is a mournful tale;
A poor blind prisoner here I am,
  In Dublin's dreary gaol;
Struck blind within the trenches,
  Where I never feared the foe;
And now I'll never see again
  My own sweet Aherlow.

A poor neglected mendicant,
  I wandered through the street;
My nine months' pension now being out,
  I beg from all I meet:
As I joined my country's tyrants,
  My face I'll never show
Among the kind old neighbours
  In the Glen of Aherlow.

Then, Irish youths, dear countrymen,
   Take heed of what I say;
For if you join the English ranks,
   You'll surely rue the day;
And whenever you are tempted
   A-soldiering to go,
Remember poor blind Sheehan
   Of the Glen of Aherlow.

CHARLES JOSEPH KICKHAM

RORY OF THE HILL

'That rake up near the rafters, why leave it there so
      long?
The handle, of the best of ash, is smooth, and straight,
      and strong;
And, mother, will you tell me, why did my father
      frown,
When to make the hay, in summer-time, I climbed to
      take it down?'
She looked into her husband's eyes, while her own with
      light did fill.
'You'll shortly know the reason, boy!' said Rory of the
      Hill.

The midnight moon is lighting up the slopes of
      Sliav-na-man,—
Whose foot affrights the startled hares so long before
      the dawn?
He stopped just where the Anner's stream winds up
      the woods anear,
Then whistled low and looked around to see the
      coast was clear.
A sheeling door flew open—in he stepped with right
      good will—
'God save all here, and bless your work,' said Rory of
      the Hill.

194

Right hearty was the welcome that greeted him, I
       ween,
For years gone by he fully proved how well he loved
       the Green;
And there was one among them who grasped him by
       the hand—
One who through all that weary time roamed on a
       foreign strand;
He brought them news from gallant friends that made
       their heart-strings thrill—
'My sowl! I never doubted them!' said Rory of the Hill.

They sat around the humble board till dawning of the
       day,
And yet not song nor shout I heard—no revellers were
       they:
Some brows flushed red with gladness, while some were
       grimly pale;
But pale or red, from out those eyes flashed souls that
       never quail!
'And sing us now about the vow, they swore for to
       fulfil'—
"You'll read it yet in History,' said Rory of the Hill.

Next day the ashen handle, he took down from where
       it hung,
The toothed rake, full scornfully, into the fire he
       flung;
And in its stead a shining blade is gleaming once
       again—
(Oh! for a hundred thousand of such weapons and such
       men!)
Right soldierly he wielded it, and, going through his
       drill,
'Attention!'—'Charge!'—'Front, point!'—'Advance!'
       cried Rory of the Hill.

She looked at him with woman's pride, with pride and
       woman's fears;

She flew to him, she clung to him, and dried away her
    tears;
He feels her pulse beat truly, while her arms around him
    twine—
'Now God be praised for your stout heart, brave little
    wife of mine.'
He swung his first-born in the air, while joy his heart
    did fill—
'You'll be a Freeman yet, my boy,' said Rory of the Hill.

Oh! knowledge is a wondrous power, and stronger than
    the wind;
And thrones shall fall, and despots bow before the might
    of mind;
The poet and the orator, the heart of man can sway,
And would to the kind heavens that Wolfe Tone were
    here to-day!
Yet trust me, friends, dear Ireland's strength, her truest
    strength, is still
The rough and ready roving boys, like Rory of the Hill.

TIMOTHY DANIEL SULLIVAN

GOD SAVE IRELAND

*William O'Meara Allen, Michael O'Brien, and Michael Larkin
were executed for accidentally killing a policeman while attempting to rescue fellow Fenians from a Manchester jail. Their deaths
were commemorated in these verses by Timothy Daniel Sullivan,
who served not only in a British prison but as Lord Mayor of
Dublin and was three times elected to the British Parliament.*

High upon the gallows tree swung the noble-hearted
    three,
    By the vengeful tyrant stricken in their bloom;
But they met him face to face, with the courage of their
    race,

And they went with souls undaunted to their doom.
"God save Ireland," said the heroes; "God save Ireland,"
    said they all:
"Whether on the scaffold high, or the battle-field we
    die,
"O what matter, when for Erin dear we fall!"

Girt around with cruel foes, still their spirit proudly rose,
    For they thought of hearts that loved them, far and
      near,
Of the millions true and brave, o'er the ocean's swelling
      wave,
    And the friends in holy Ireland, ever dear.
"God save Ireland," said they proudly; "God save
    Ireland," said they all:
"Whether on the scaffold high, or the battle-field we die,
"Oh what matter, when for Erin dear we fall!"

Climbed they up the rugged stair; rung their voices out
    in prayer;
    Then, with England's fatal cord around them cast,
Close beneath the gallows tree, kissed like brothers
    lovingly,
    True to home and faith and freedom to the last.
"God save Ireland," prayed they loudly; "God save
    Ireland," said they all:
"Whether on the scaffold high, or the battle-field we die,
"O what matter, when for Erin dear we fall!"

Never till the latest day shall the memory pass away
    Of the gallant lives thus given for our land;
But on the cause must go, amidst joy, or weal or woe,
    Till we've made our isle a nation free and grand.
"God save Ireland," say we proudly; "God save Ireland,"
    say we all:
"Whether on the scaffold high, or the battle-field we
    die,
"O what matter, when for Erin dear we fall!"

BY MEMORY INSPIRED

By memory inspired,
And love of country fired,
The deeds of men I love to dwell upon;
And the patriotic glow
Of my spirit must bestow
A tribute to O'Connell that is gone, boys—gone:
Here's a memory to the friends that are gone!

In October Ninety-seven—
May his soul find rest in Heaven!—
William Orr to execution was led on:
The jury, drunk, agreed
That Irish was his creed;
For perjury and threats drove them on, boys—on:
Here's the memory of John Mitchell that is gone!

In Ninety-eight—the month July—
The informer's pay was high;
When Reynolds gave the gallows brave MacCann;
But MacCann was Reynold's first—
One could not allay his thirst;
So he brought up Bond and Byrne, that are gone, boys—
      gone:
Here's the memory of the friends that are gone!

We saw a nation's tears
Shed for John and Henry Shears;
Betrayed by Judas, Captain Armstrong;
We may forgive, but yet
We never can forget
The poisoning of Maguire that is gone, boys—gone:
Our high Star and true Apostle that is gone!

How did Lord Edward die?
Like a man, without a sigh;

But he left his handiwork on Major Swan!
  But Sirr, with steel-clad breast,
  And coward heart at best,
Left us cause to mourn Lord Edward that is gone, boys—
        gone:
Here's the memory of our friends that are gone!
  September Eighteen-three,
  Closed this cruel history,
When Emmet's blood the scaffold flowed upon:
  Oh, had their spirits been wise,
  They might then realize
Their freedom! But we drink to Mitchell that is gone,
        boys—gone:
Here's the memory of the friends that are gone!

FANNY PARNELL

AFTER DEATH

Fanny Parnell (1854-1882), sister of Charles Stewart Parnell, began contributing patriotic verses to Irish publications before she reached her teens. Later she helped organize the Land League and made speeches for her brother's cause.

Shall mine eyes behold thy glory, O my country?
  Shall mine eyes behold thy glory?
Or shall the darkness close around them, ere the
      sunblaze
  Break at last upon thy story?

When the nations ope for thee their queenly circle,
  As a sweet new sister hail thee,
Shall these lips be sealed in callous death and silence,
  That have known but to bewail thee?

Shall the ear be deaf that only loved thy praises,
  When all men their tribute bring thee?

Shall the mouth be clay that sang thee in thy squalor,
  When all poets' mouths shall sing thee?

Ah! the harpings and the salvos and the shoutings
  Of thy exiled sons returning!
I should hear, tho' dead and mouldered, and the
          grave-damps
  Should not chill my bosom's burning.

Ah! the tramp of feet victorious! I should hear them
  'Mid the shamrocks and the mosses,
And my heart should toss within the shroud and quiver,
  As a captive dreamer tosses.

I should turn and rend the cere-clothes round me,
  Giant sinews I should borrow—
Crying, "O, my brothers, I have also loved her
  In her loneliness and sorrow!

"Let me join with you the jubilant procession;
  Let me chant with you her story;
Then contented I shall go back to the shamrocks,
  Now mine eyes have seen her glory!"

For centuries Irish revolts against English rule had relied heavily on help promised by England's foes on the Continent— France and Spain. Such assistance was either inadequate or did not come at all. Not until the philosophy of the following poem was accepted did Ireland win freedom. The Gaelic for "Ourselves Alone" is "Sinn Fein"—and it was Sinn Fein, not foreign aid, that established the Irish Republic of today.

OURSELVES ALONE

John O'Hagan (1822-1890) contributed these verses to The
Nation *shortly after his graduation from Trinity College. He
became a leading member of the Young Ireland Party and was
appointed by Gladstone the first judicial head of the Irish Land
Commission.*

The work that should to-day be wrought,
  Defer not till to-morrow;
The help that should within be sought
  Scorn from without to borrow.
Old maxims these—yet stout and true—
  They speak in trumpet tone,
To do at once what is to do,
  And trust OURSELVES ALONE.

Too long our Irish hearts we schooled
  In patient hope to bide,
By dreams of English justice fooled
  And English tongues that lied.
That hour of weak delusion's past—
  The empty dream has flown:
Our hope and strength, we find at last,
  Is in OURSELVES ALONE.

Aye! bitter hate or cold neglect,
  Or lukewarm love at best,
Is all we've found, or can expect,
  We aliens of the West.
No friend, beyond our own green shore,
  Can Erin truly own;
Yet stronger is her trust, therefore,
  In her brave sons ALONE.

Remember when our lot was worse—
  Sunk, trampled to the dust—

'Twas long our weakness and our curse
  In stranger aid to trust.
And if, at length, we proudly trod
  On bigot laws o'erthrown,
Who won that struggle? Under God,
  Ourselves—OURSELVES ALONE.

Oh! let its memory be enshrined
  In Ireland's heart forever!
It proves a banded people's mind
  Must win in just endeavor;
It shows how wicked to despair,
  How weak to idly groan—
If ills at *other's* hands ye bear,
  The cure is in YOUR OWN.

The foolish word "impossible"
  At once, for aye, disdain!
No power can bar a people's will,
  A people's right to gain.
Be bold, united, firmly set,
  Nor flinch in word or tone—
We'll be a glorious nation yet,
  REDEEMED—ERECT—ALONE!

Lord Thomas Babington Macaulay, British Secretary for War under Lord Melbourne, summarized the Irish problem as follows:

We have used the sword for centuries against the Irish; we have tried famine, we have tried extermination, we have had recourse to all the severity of the law. What have we done? Have we succeeded? We have been able neither to exterminate nor enfeeble them. I confess my incapacity to solve this problem. They must be on the rock of St. Peter that the gates of hell shall not prevail against them.

EASTER WEEK, 1916

When England found herself at war with Germany in 1914, the British Parliament rushed through a Home Rule Act such as Irishmen had long been fighting for. But it was not to take effect until after the war. This act, plus sympathy for invaded Belgium, caused great numbers of Irishmen to volunteer for service in the British army. The percentage of the population of Ireland that volunteered to fight in World War I was comparable to the percentage of Americans who served after being drafted. More Irish died than Belgians.

Thomas Kettle, a member of the secret Irish Revolutionary Brotherhood and of Sinn Fein, was in Belgium buying arms to fight the British when the Germans invaded. He was so shocked by what he considered a threat to Christian civilization that he hurried home and amazed his rebel friends by enlisting in the British Army. In a poem entitled "The Last Crusade" he wrote:

> Then lift the flag of the last Crusade!
> And fill the ranks of the Last Brigade!
> March on to the fields where the world's re-made,
> And the ancient Dreams come true!

The evening before he died leading his Dublin Fusileers in a bloody capture of supposedly impregnable German trenches, he wrote these verses:

THOMAS KETTLE

TO MY DAUGHTER, BETTY

—the Gift of God

In wiser days, my darling rosebud, blown
To beauty proud as was your mother's prime,
In that desired, delayed incredible time,
You'll ask why I deserted you my own,
And the dear heart that was your baby throne
To dice with death. And, O! they'll give you rhyme
And reason: some will call the thing sublime
And some decry it in a knowing tone.

So here, while the mad guns curse overhead
And tired men sigh with mud for couch and floor
Know that we fools, now with the foolish dead,
Died not for flag, nor King, nor Emperor,
But for a dream, born in a herdsman's shed,
And for the secret Scripture of the poor.

Although half a million Irishmen fought in British armies, there were three organizations at home that felt that the Home Rule Act was a fraud (as it was), never to be implemented. After the third postponement of implementation, the Irish Republican Brotherhood, the Irish Volunteers, and the Irish Citizens Army began to prepare for action. Sir Roger Casement was to bring arms and ammunition from Germany to equip the three groups for a nationwide uprising immediately following Easter.

But the ship was intercepted by the British before it could land its cargo on the West Coast, and its crew sank it to prevent British capture of the weapons it carried. Some of the crew were drowned; others, including Casement, were imprisoned by the British.

This disaster caused Eoin MacNeil, head of the Irish Volunteers, to countermand previous orders and instruct his group to take no action on Easter Monday. But other leaders, partic-

ularly in Dublin, decided to fight—no matter the odds, no matter how hopeless of victory.

At noon on Easter Monday, 1916, Patrick Henry Pearse, as Provisional President and Commandant-General, proclaimed the Irish Republic from the foot of Nelson's Pillar in the heart of Dublin. As he read, rebels were taking over the General Post Office, railway stations, the Four Courts, and other strategic spots in Dublin and suburbs.

The rebels had fewer than 1,800 rifles and little ammunition. Britain had four million men in arms, 20,000 of whom were in Dublin by Tuesday morning. These soldiers were supplied with unlimited rifles, machine guns, and artillery. A gunboat came up the Liffey to the center of Dublin to shell both sides of the river. Whole blocks of buildings burned down.

For five full days the rebels held out. But by Saturday their ammunition had been exhausted. Pearse and the other leaders signed an unconditional surrender.

Secret courts-martial were swiftly held and the leaders were promptly executed. After being encased in quicklime, their bodies were buried in unmarked graves so that future generations might never have even a bone for a relic of them. Six thousand men and women were seized from their homes and transported without trial to English prisons.

Sir John Maxwell, commander-in-chief of the British forces in Ireland, then proudly announced that he had "stamped out rebellion for all time in Ireland."

The ideals for which Thomas Kettle died were not implemented by the British government in Ireland. Among the Irishmen who correctly suspected that the Home Rule Act would never go into effect were three close friends of Kettle, Joseph Mary Plunkett (1887-1916), Thomas MacDonagh, and Patrick Henry Pearse. All three were poets, all three were leaders in the brief rising of Easter Week, and all three were shot by the British after their surrender. Plunkett was allowed to marry Grace Gifford, sister of the wife of Thomas MacDonagh, in the prison barracks the night before he was shot. One of his poems follows:

JOSEPH MARY PLUNKETT

OUR HERITAGE

This heritage to the race of Kings:
Their children and their children's seed
Have wrought their prophecies in deed
Of terrible and splendid things.

The hands that fought, the hearts that broke
In old immortal tragedies,
These have not failed beneath the skies,
Their children's heads refuse the yoke.

And still their hands shall guard the sod
That holds their father's funeral urn,
Still shall their hearts volcanic burn
With anger of the Sons of God.

No alien sword shall earn as wage
The entail of their blood and tears,
No shameful price for peaceful years
Shall ever part this heritage.

Another poem by Plunkett ended with these words:

> *Because I know the spark*
> *Of God has no eclipse,*
> *Now Death and I embark,*
> *And sail into the dark*
> *With laughter on our lips.*

WISHES FOR MY SON

Born on St. Cecilia's Day—1912

Tom MacDonagh was a kindly, lovable fellow who started out to become a priest. But he married and was devoted to his family. He wrote and spoke Latin, French, and Gaelic. He was a professor of English at the National University (where Kettle was professor of economics) when he wrote these two prophetic poems:

Now, my son, is life for you—
And I wish you joy of it—
Joy of power in all you do,
Deeper passion, better wit
Than I had who had enough,
Quicker life and length thereof,
More of every gift but love.

Love I have beyond all men,
Love that now you share with me—
What have I to wish you then
But that you be good and free,
And that God to you may give
Grace in stronger days to live?

For I wish you more than I
Ever knew of glorious deed,
Though no rapture passed me by
That an eager heart could heed,
Though I followed heights and sought
Things the sequel never brought.

Wild and perilous holy things
Flaming with a martyr's blood,
And the joy that laughs and sings
Where a foe must be withstood,

Joy of headlong happy chance
Leading on the battle dance.

But I found no enemy,
No man in a world of wrong,
That Christ's word of Charity
Did not render clean and strong—
Who was I to judge my kind,
Blindest groper of the blind?

God to you may give the sight
And the clear undoubting strength
Wars to knit for single right,
Fredom's war to knit at length
And to win, through wrath and strife,
To the sequel of my life.

But for you, so small and young,
Born on St. Cecilia's Day,
I in more harmonious song
Now for nearer joys should pray—
Simple joys: the natural growth
Of your childhood and your youth,
Courage, innocence and truth:

These for you, so small and young
In your hand and heart and tongue.

The son, Donagh MacDonagh, is now a judge in Ireland and a poet of distinction.

THOMAS MACDONAGH

ON A POET PATRIOT

His songs were a little phrase
Of eternal song,

Drowned in the harping of lays
  More loud and long.

His deed was a single word,
  Called out alone
In a night when no echo stirred
  To laughter or moan.

But his songs new souls shall thrill,
  The loud harps dumb,
And his deed the echoes fill
  When the dawn is come.

Patrick Henry Pearse (1879-1916) was the son of a Protestant Englishman and an Irish mother. He was a devout Catholic and no more dedicated Irishman ever lived. He founded and operated two unique schools—St. Edna's for boys and St. Ita's for girls. They were Catholic but with lay teachers. Displayed over a mural in the reception room of the boys' school were the words of a Gaelic hero:

> *I care not if my life have only the span of a night and a day if my deeds be spoken of by the men of Ireland.*

Others executed included William Pearse, a sculptor and brother of Patrick, and John MacBride, whose son, Sean Mac-Bride, has had a most successful career in Ireland and internationally.

Following are five poems by Pearse, the first three clearly prophetic. The first, "Ideal," was written in Gaelic and translated by MacDonagh.

IDEAL

Naked I saw thee,
O beauty of beauty!
And I blinded my eyes
For fear I should flinch.

I heard thy music,
O sweetness of sweetness!
And I shut my ears
For fear I should fail.

I kissed thy lips,
O sweetness of sweetness!
And I hardened my heart
For fear of my ruin.

I blinded my eyes
And my ears I shut,
I hardened my heart
And my love I quenched.

I turned my back
On the dream I had shaped,
And to this road before me
My face I turned.

I set my face
To the road here before me,
To the work that I see,
To the death that I shall meet.

THE REBEL

I come of the seed of the people, the people that
     sorrow,
That have no treasure but hope,
No riches laid up but a memory
Of an ancient glory.
My mother bore me in bondage, in bondage my mother
     was born,
I am the blood of serfs;
The children with whom I have played, the men and
     women with whom I have eaten,
Have had masters over them, they have been under the
     lash of masters,
And, though gentle, have served churls;
The hands that have touched mine, the dear hands
     whose touch is familiar to me,
Have worn shameful manacles, have been bitten at the
     wrist by manacles,
Have grown hard with the manacles and the task-work
     of strangers,
I am flesh of the flesh of these lowly, I am bone of their
     bone,
I have never submitted;
I that have a soul greater than the souls of my people's
     masters,
I have vision and prophecy and the gift of fiery speech,
I that have spoken with God on the top of His holy hill.
And because I am of the people, I understand the
     people,
I am sorrowful with their sorrow, I am hungry with
     their desire:
My heart has been heavy with the grief of mothers,
My eyes have been wet with the tears of children,
I have yearned with old wistful men,
And laughed or cursed with young men;

Their shame is my shame, and I have reddened for it.
Reddened for that they have gone in want, while others
        have been full,
Reddened for that they have walked in fear of lawyers
        and of their jailors
With their writs of summons and their handcuffs,
Men mean and cruel!
I could have borne stripes on my body rather than this
        shame of my people.
I say to my people that they are holy, that they are
        august, despite their chains,
That they are greater than those that hold them, and
        stronger and purer,
That they have but need of courage, and to call on the
        name of their God,
God the unforgetting, the dear God that loves the
        peoples For whom He died naked, suffering
        shame.
And I say to my people's masters: Beware,
Beware of the thing that is coming, beware of the risen
        people,
Who shall take what ye would not give. Did ye think
        to conquer the people,
Or that Law is stronger than life and than men's desire
        to be free?
We will try it out with you, ye that have harried and
        held,
Ye that have bullied and bribed, tyrants, hypocrites,
        liars!

PATRICK HENRY PEARSE

THE FOOL

Since the wise men have not spoken, I speak that am
        only a fool;

A fool that has loved his folly,
Yea, more than the wise men their books or their
      counting houses, or their quiet homes,
Or their fame in men's mouths;
A fool that in all his days hath done never a prudent
      thing,
Never hath counted the cost, nor recked if another
      reaped
The fruit of his mighty sowing, content to scatter the
      seed;
A fool that is unrepentant, and that soon at the end of
      all
Shall laugh in his lonely heart as the ripe ears fall to
      the reaping-hooks
And the poor are filled that were empty,
Tho' he go hungry.
I have squandered the splendid years that the Lord God
      gave to my youth
In attempting impossible things, deeming them alone
      worth the toil.
Was it folly or grace? Not men shall judge me, but
      God.
I have squandered the splendid years:
Lord, if I had the years I would squander them over
      again,
Aye, fling them from me!
For this I have heard in my heart, that a man shall
      scatter, not hoard,
Shall do the deed of to-day, nor take thought of
      to-morrow's teen,
Shall not bargain or huxter with God; or was it a jest
      of Christ's
And is this my sin before men, to have taken Him at
      His word?

The lawyers have sat in council, the men with the keen,
      long faces,
And said, "This man is a fool," and others have said,

213

"He blasphemeth;"
And the wise have pitied the fool that hath striven to
    give a life
In the world of time and space among the bulks of
    actual things,
To a dream that was dreamed in the heart, and that
    only the heart could hold.

O wise men, riddle me this: what if the dream come
    true?
What if the dream come true? and if millions unborn
    shall dwell
In the house that I shaped in my heart, the noble house
    of my thought?
Lord, I have staked my soul, I have staked the lives of
    my kin
On the truth of Thy dreadful word. Do not remember
    my failures,
But remember this my faith.

And so I speak.
Yea, ere my hot youth pass, I speak to my people and
    say:
Ye shall be foolish as I; ye shall scatter, not save;
Ye shall venture your all, lest ye lose what is more than
    all;
Ye shall call for a miracle, taking Christ at His word.
And for this I will answer, O people, answer here and
    hereafter,
O people that I have loved shall we not answer
    together?

*When Pearse was condemned to death his mother asked him
to write a poem specially for her. The night before he was shot
Pearse wrote two poems, the first in the form of a prayer by his
mother to the Blessed Virgin.*

214

Dear Mary, thou didst see thy first-born Son
Go forth to die amid the scorn of men
For whom He died.
Receive my first-born son into thy arms,
And keep him by thee till I come to him.
Dear Mary, I have shared thy sorrow
And soon will share thy joy.

The second poem was also in the form of a prayer.

PATRICK HENRY PEARSE

THE MOTHER

I do not grudge them; Lord, I do not grudge
My two strong sons that I have seen go out
To break their strength and die, they and a few,
In bloody protest for a glorious thing.
They shall be spoken of among their people,
The generations shall remember them,
And call them blessed;
But I will speak their names to my own heart
In the long nights;
The little names that were familiar once
Round my dead hearth.
Lord, thou art hard on mothers:
We suffer in their coming and their going;
And tho' I grudge them not, I weary, weary
Of the long sorrow—And yet I have my joy:
My sons were faithful, and they fought.

The execution of James Connolly had been delayed a few
days. He had received one bullet in the arm and another had
shattered a leg. The British wanted to shoot him while he stood

against a wall, but he could not stand. Finally they took him from the hospital on a stretcher, propped him up, and shot him.

Connolly was known not as a poet but as a Socialist Labor leader. He had spent several years in the United States and while here published a book of verse. Shortly before his return to Ireland, against the wishes of his wife (they had eight children), he wrote this explanation of his action:

> Glorious is the land we're leaving
> And its pride shall grow with years,
> And the land which calls us homeward
> Can but share with us her tears.
> Yet our heart her call obeying
> Heedless of the wealth men crave,
> Turneth home to share her sorrow,
> Where she weeps beside the wave.
>
> She is calling, she is calling in the wind
> And o'er the tide.
> We, her children, hear her voices
> Call us ever to her side.

Constance Gore-Booth, Countess de Markievicz, commanded a detachment of the rebels. She was imprisoned after the surrender. One of her poems follows.

CONSTANCE DE MARKIEVICZ

A BATTLE HYMN

Armed for the battle, kneel we before Thee,
Bless Thou our banners, God of the brave!
Ireland is living! shout we exultant;
Ireland is waking, hands grasp the sword.
Who fights for Ireland, God guide his blows home
Who dies for Ireland, God give him peace!
Knowing our just cause, march we triumphant.
Living or dying. Ireland to free.

The spirit of freedom floats in the ether,
Souls of our heroes march by our side,
Tone is our battle-cry: Emmet inspires us;
Those who for freedom fall never shall die.
England is breaking! shout we exultant;
England is beaten! Ireland is free!
Charge for the old cause; down with the old foe!
Giving our heart's blood Ireland to free!

After the rising of a few hundred rebels had been smashed
by twenty thousand British troops and heavy artillery, and
after the sixteen leaders who surrendered had been shot, there
was much criticism of the revolt—even from patriotic Irishmen.
It seemed to have been a complete and utter failure. A charitable
view was expressed by an anonymous poet in a Dublin paper.

ANONYMOUS

THE DUBLIN EXECUTIONS

Pray every man in his abode
    And let the church bells toll,
For those who did not know the road,
    But only saw the goal.

Let there be weeping in the land,
    And Charity of mind
For those who did not understand,
    Because their love was blind.

Their errant scheme that we condemn,
    All perished at a touch;
But much should be forgiven them
    Because they loved much.

Let no harsh tongue applaud their fate,
    Or their clean names decry;

The men who had no strength to wait,
    But only strength to die.

Come all ye to their requiem
    Who gave all men can give,
And be ye slow to follow them,
    And hasty to forgive.

And let each man in his abode
    Pray for each dead man's soul,
Of those who did not know the road,
    But only saw the goal.

Many poets in Ireland, England, and the United States were inspired to comment, but not one of them realized what the dead men had accomplished.

Theodore Maynard, the English poet, wrote of Pearse:

> *By one who walks aloof in English ways*
> *Be this high word of praise and sorrow said:*
> *He lived in honor all his lovely days,*
> *And is immortal, dead.*

Msgr. Padraig de Brun put it this way:

> *And though this idle tribute of our tears*
> *We pay to those who fell, we know 'tis vain,*
> *For they have died with proud unflinching gaze,*
> *Glad that in death they wiped away the stain*
> *Of servitude that marked us in the ways*
> *Of past disgraceful years,*
> *And linked our time to ages long ago,*
> *And chiefs who never to false altars bowed,*
> *Whom gifts had never won nor threats had cowed,*
> *Emmett and Tone, Sarsfield and Owen Roe.*

Countess Constance de Markievicz commanded a detachment of fighters in the rising. Following the surrender she was sentenced to life imprisonment at hard labor. Her sister, Eva Gore-Booth, summarized her feelings in these lines:

> All flowers fade as the years onward roll,
> Theirs is a deathless wreath—a crown of thorns.

This was the tribute of James Stephens:

> Be green upon their graves, O happy Spring!
> For they were young and eager who are dead!
> Of all things that are young, and quivering
> With eager life, be they remembered!
> They move not here! They have gone to the clay!
> They cannot die again for liberty!
> Be they remembered of their land for aye!
> Green be their graves, and green their memory!

Dora Sigerson Shorter

SIXTEEN DEAD MEN

Dora Sigerson Shorter (1866-1918), whose husband was editor of the Illustrated London News, wrote of the fifteen men who were shot and of Roger Casement, who was hung a few months later.

> Hark! in the still night. Who goes there?
>   "Fifteen dead men." Why do they wait?
> "Hasten, comrade, death is so fair."
>   Now comes their Captain through the dim gate.
>
> Sixteen dead men! What on their sword?
>   "A nation's honour proud do they bear."
> What on their bent heads? "God's holy word;
>   All of their nation's heart blended in prayer."

Sixteen dead men! What makes their shroud?
  "All of their nation's love wraps them around."
Where do their bodies lie, brave and so proud?
  "Under the gallows-tree in prison ground."

Sixteen dead men! Where do they go?
  "To join their regiment, where Sarsfield leads;
Wolfe Tone and Emmett, too, well do they know.
  There they shall bivouac, telling great deeds."

Sixteen dead men! Shall they return?
  "Yea, they shall come again, breath of our breath.
They on our nation's hearth made old fires burn.
  Guard her unconquered soul, strong in their death."

*Lady Gregory, in her poem "The Old Woman Remembers,"
reviews seven hundred years of Irish rebellions, culminating in
this verse:*

> *In Easter Week the wisp was lit*
> *Waked Dublin from her drowsy years;*
> *I moan the battle-anger, yet*
> *What did we ever win by tears?*
> *The ballad singers long have cried*
> *The shining names of far-away;*
> *Now let them rhyme out those that died*
> *With the three-colors yesterday.*

*Dermot O'Byrne, in "A Dublin Ballad—1916," expressed shame
that he had not participated in the rising. His final lines were:*

> *Well, the last fire is trodden down,*
> *Our dead are rotting fast in lime,*
> *We all can sneak back into town,*
> *Stravague about as in old time,*
>
> *And stare at gaps of grey and blue*
> *Where Lower Mount Street used to be,*

And where flies hum round muck we knew
For Abbey Street and Eden Quay.

And when the devil's made us wise
Each in his own peculiar hell,
With desert hearts and drunken eyes
We're free to sentimentalize
By corners where the martyrs fell.

Francis Ledwidge (1891-1917) paid this tribute to Thomas MacDonagh:

He shall not hear the bittern cry
In the wild sky, where he is lain,
Nor voices of the sweeter birds
Above the wailing of the rain.

Nor shall he know when loud March blows
Thro' slanting snows her fanfare shrill,
Blowing to flame the golden cup
Of many an upset daffodil.

But when the Dark Cow leaves the moor,
And pastures poor with greedy weeds,
Perhaps he'll hear her low at morn
Lifting her horn in pleasant meads.

George William Russell (1867-1935), better known as A. E., had not approved the rising, but he wrote "Salutation":

Your dream had left me numb and cold
But yet my spirit rose in pride,
Re-fashioning in burnished gold
The images of those who died,
Or were shut in the penal cell—
Here's to you, Pearse, your dream, not mine,
But yet the thought—for this you fell—
Turns all life's water into wine.

I listened to high talk from you,
Thomas MacDonagh, and it seemed
The words were idle, but they grew
To nobleness, by death redeemed.
Life cannot utter things more great
Than life can meet with sacrifice,
High words were equalled by high fate,
You paid the price. You paid the price.

The hope lives on, age after age,
Earth with her beauty might be won
For labor as a heritage—
For this has Ireland lost a son,
This hope into a flame to fan
Men have put life by with a smile.
Here's to you, Connolly, my man,
Who cast the last torch on the pile.

Here's to the women of our race
Stood by them in the fiery hour,
Rapt, lest some weakness in their blood
Rob manhood of a single power—
You, brave as such a hope forlorn,
Who smiled through crack of shot and shell,
Though the world look on you with scorn,
Here's to you, Constance,[1] in your cell.

Here's to you, men I never met,
But hope to meet behind the veil,
Thronged on some starry parapet
That looks down upon Inisfail,
And see the confluence of dreams
That clashed together in our night,
One river born of many streams
Roll in one blaze of blinding light!

---

[1] Countess Constance de Markievicz.

222

When John O'Leary, the great Fenian leader, died in 1913, William Butler Yeats, who had once been a member of the Irish Revolutionary Brotherhood, wrote:

Romantic Ireland's dead and gone.
It's with O'Leary in his grave.

The response of Yeats to Easter Week was awaited with great interest. From the battlefields of France, Joyce Kilmer, the American poet, addressed this question to Yeats:

"Romantic Ireland's dead and gone.
It's with O'Leary in his grave."
Then, Yeats, what gave that Easter dawn
A hue so radiantly brave?

There is no rope can strangle song
And not for long death takes his toll.
No prison bars can dim the stars
Nor quicklime eat the living soul.

Romantic Ireland is not old.
For years untold her youth will shine,
Her heart is fed on Heavenly bread,
The blood of martyrs is her wine.

Yeats responded with these verses:

WILLIAM BUTLER YEATS

EASTER 1916

I have met them at close of day
Coming with vivid faces
From counter or desk among grey
Eighteenth-century houses.

I have passed with a nod of the head
Or polite meaningless words,
Or have lingered awhile and said
Polite meaningless words,
And thought before I had done
Of a mocking tale or a gibe
To please a companion
Around the fire at the club,
Being certain that they and I
But lived where motley is worn:
All changed, changed utterly:
A terrible beauty is born.

That woman's days were spent
In ignorant good will,
Her nights in argument
Until her voice grew shrill.
What voice more sweet than hers
When young and beautiful,
She rode to harriers?
This man had kept a school
And rode our winged horse;
This other his helper and friend
Was coming into his force;
He might have won fame in the end,
So sensitive his nature seemed,
So daring and sweet his thought.
This other man I had dreamed
A drunken, vainglorious lout.
He had done most bitter wrong
To some who are near my heart,
Yet I number him in the song;
He, too, has resigned his part
In the casual comedy;
He, too, has been changed in his turn,
Transformed utterly:
A terrible beauty is born.

Hearts with one purpose alone
Through summer and winter seem
Enchanted to a stone
To trouble the living stream.
The horse that comes from the road,
The rider, the birds that range
From cloud to tumbling cloud,
Minute by minute they change;
A shadow of cloud on the stream
Changes minute by minute;
A horse-hoof slides on the brim,
And a horse plashes within it
Where long-legged moorhens dive,
And hens to moorcocks call.
Minute by minute they live:
The stone's in the midst of all.

Too long a sacrifice
Can make a stone of the heart.
O when may it suffice?
That is heaven's part, our part
To murmur name upon name,
As a mother names her child
When sleep at last has come
On limbs that had run wild.
What is it but nightfall?
No, no, not night but death;
Was it needless death after all?
For England may keep faith
For all that is done and said.
We know their dream; enough
To know they dreamed and are dead;
And what if excess of love
Bewildered them till they died?
I write it out in a verse—
MacDonagh and MacBride
And Connolly and Pearse

Now and in time to be,
Wherever green is worn,
Are changed, changed utterly:
A terrible beauty is born.

WILLIAM BUTLER YEATS

THE ROSE TREE

"O words lightly spoken"
Said Pearse to Connolly,
"Maybe a breath of politic words
Has withered our Rose Tree;
Or maybe but a wind that blows
Across the bitter sea."

"It needs to be but watered,"
James Connolly replied,
"To make the green come out again
And spread on every side,
And shake the blossom from the bud
To be the garden's pride."

"But where can we draw water,"
Said Pearse to Connolly,
"When all the wells are parched away?
O plain as plain can be
There's nothing but our own red blood
Can make a right Rose Tree."

SIXTEEN DEAD MEN

O but we talked at large before
The sixteen men were shot,
But who can talk of give and take,
What should be and what not
While those dead men are loitering there
To stir the boiling pot?

You say that we should still the land
Till Germany's overcome;
But who is there to argue that
Now Pearse is deaf and dumb?
And is their logic to outweigh
MacDonagh's bony thumb?

How could you dream they'd listen
That have an ear alone
For the new comrades they have found,
Lord Edward and Wolfe Tone,
Or meddle with our give and take
That converse bone to bone?

These anonymous lines, which appeared in a Dublin news-paper, probably best expressed the popular reaction to Easter Week:

ANONYMOUS

EASTER WEEK

(The Song of 1916)

Who fears to speak of Easter Week,
Who dares its fate deplore?
The red-gold flame of Erin's name
Confronts the world once more.

So Irishmen remember them
  And raise your heads with pride,
That great men, and straight men,
  Have fought for you and died.

The storied page of this, our age,
  Will save our land from shame;
The ancient foe had boasted low
  That Irishmen were tame.

They'd bought their souls with paltry doles,
  They told the world of slaves,
That lie, men, will die, men,
  In Pearse and Plunkett's graves.

GOD SAVE IRELAND

Following the executions, George Bernard Shaw issued this widely quoted statement:

. . . the men who were shot in cold blood after their capture or surrender, were prisoners of war, and it was entirely incorrect to slaughter them. The relation of Ireland to Dublin Castle is, in this respect, precisely that of the Balkan States to Turkey, of Belgium or the city of Lille to the Kaiser, and of the United States to Great Britain.

Until Dublin Castle is superseded by a National Parliament and Ireland voluntarily incorporated with the British Empire, as Canada, Australasia, and South Africa have been incorporated, an Irishman resorting to arms to achieve the independence of his country is doing only what Englishmen will do if it be their misfortune to be invaded and conquered by the Germans in the course of the present war.

Further, such an Irishman is as much in order morally in accepting assistance from the Germans in his struggle with England, as England is in accepting the assistance of Russia in her struggle with Germany. The fact that he knows that his enemies will not respect his rights if they catch him, and that he must, therefore, fight with a rope around his neck, increases his risk, but adds in the same measure to his glory in the eyes of his compatriots and of the disinterested admirers of patriotism throughout the world. It is absolutely impossible to slaughter a man in this position without making him a martyr and a hero, even though the day before the rising he may have been only a minor poet. The shot Irishmen will now take their places beside Emmett and the Manchester Martyrs in Ireland, and beside the heroes of Poland and Serbia and Belgium in Europe; and nothing in Heaven or earth can prevent it. . . .

I remain an Irishman, and am bound to contradict any implication that I can regard as a traitor any Irishman taken in a fight for Irish Independence against the British Government, which was a fair fight in everything except the enormous odds my countrymen had to face.

The dramatic result of Easter Week could not have been foreseen. Desmond Ryan characterized it as "the most arresting and indubitable example in all history of the triumph of failure." When the prisoners were shot it was announced that the speed and ferocity of the punishment were regretted by the government but were necessary to "stamp out rebellion completely and permanently." But the men of Easter Week, who had only a few followers when alive, by their words and deaths fused and welded the people of Ireland into a unity and determination such as they had never known.

Six years after their failure Ireland had independence.

The men who had joined Tom Kettle in fighting England's battles had their part in the final victory. On every battlefield of a World War they learned well the arts of war and the trade of

killing. They returned to find that there was to be no imple-
mentation of the Home Rule Act that had lured them into
service. The bodies of the men of Easter Week had been covered
with quicklime and cast without coffins into unmarked pits so
that they might be forgotten. But their words and their deeds
lived on. The foolish Easter rising of 1916 flowered in the glo-
rious victory of 1922.

Peter Kearney (1883-1942), who fought under Thomas Mac-
Donagh in the Easter Week rising, wrote a song for his fellow
rebels. Known as "The Soldier's Song," it has replaced "The
Wearing of the Green" as the Irish national anthem.

PETER KEARNEY

THE SOLDIER'S SONG

We'll sing a song, a soldier's song,
With cheering rousing chorus,
As round our blazing fires we throng
The starry heavens o'er us:
Impatient for the coming fight,
And as we wait the morning's light,
Here in the silence of the night,
We'll chant a soldier's song.

CHORUS:

Soldiers are we, whose lives are pledged to Ireland;
Some have come from a land beyond the wave;
Sworn to be free, no more our ancient sireland
Shall shelter the despot or the slave.
Tonight we'll man the Bearna Boaghail.
In Erin's cause, come woe or weal,
'Mid cannon's roar or rifle's peal,
We'll chant a soldier's song.

In valleys green and towering crag
Our fathers fought before us,
And conquered 'neath the same old flag
That's proudly floating o'er us.
We're children of a fighting race,
That never yet has known disgrace.
And as we march the foe to face
We'll chant a soldier's song.

Sons of the Gael, men of the Pale,
The long-watched day is breaking;
The serried hosts of Innisfail
Shall set the tyrant quaking:
Our camp-fires now are burning low,
See, in the East a silvery glow,
Out yonder waits the Saxon foe,
So chant a soldier's song.

More than one hundred years ago, Thomas Davis wrote:

May Ireland's voice be ever heard
  Amid the world's applause!
And never be her flagstaff stirred,
  But in an honest cause!
May Freedom be her very breath,
  Be Justice ever dear;
And never an ennobled death
  May son of Ireland fear!
So the Lord God will ever smile,
  With guardian grace upon our isle.

INDEX OF FIRST LINES

233

Health and long life to you, 17
Here's to the maiden of bashful fifteen, 109
High upon the gallows tree swung the noble-hearted three, 196
His songs were a little phrase, 208
How vastly pleasing is my tale, 136

I arise to-day, 5
I charge you, lady young and fair, 110
I come to the seed of the people, the people that sorrow, 211
I do not grudge them; Lord, I do not grudge, 215
I dreamt last night of you, John-John, 61
I found in Inisfail the fair, 10
I give my heart to thee, O mother-land, 47
I have met them at close of day, 223
I love you, and I love you, and I love you, O my honey!, 90
I sailed in me foine new hooker, 95
I sit beside my darling's grave, 46
I wear a shamrock in my heart, 31
I will arise and go now, and go to Innisfree, 33
I would not give my Irish wife for all the dames of the Saxon land, 15
If you would like to see the height of hospitality, 53
I'm sittin on the stile, Mary, 158
I'm very happy where I am, 162
In a quiet water'd land of roses, 7
In Dublin's fair city, 116
In wiser days, my darling rosebud, blown, 204

Kathleen Mavourneen! the gray dawn is breaking, 112

Lesbia hath a beaming eye, 105
Let Bacchus' sons be not dismayed, 118
Let Erin remember the days of old, 19
Long they pine in weary woe, the nobles of our land, 26

Mam, dear, did ye never hear of pretty Molly Brannigan?, 120
May Ireland's voice be ever heard, 231
My eyelids red and heavy are, 59
My name is Nell, right candid I tell, 131
My name is Patrick Sheehan, 193

Naked I saw thee, 210
Nay, if flowers *will* lose their looks, 107
Not far from old Kinvara, in the merry month of May, 95
Now let me alone, though I know you won't, 99
Now with the coming in of the spring the days will stretch a bit, 35

O but we talked at large before, 227
O did you not hear of Kate Kearney?, 93
O I'm not myself at all, Molly dear, Molly dear, I'm not myself at all, 102
O my Dark Rosaleen, 23
O, the days of the Kerry dancing, O, the ring of the piper's tune!, 64

INDEX OF AUTHORS AND OTHERS

237